88/12

THE
SUFFOLK SANDLINGS

By the same author:
Over Snape Bridge (1957)
Woodbridge & Beyond (1972)
East Coast Sail (1972)
Scottish Sail (1974)
North East Sail (1976)
British Sail (1977)
Victorian & Edwardian Yachting from Old Photographs (1978)
Gaff Sail (1979)
Traditions of East Anglia (1980)
Suffolk Show (1981)
Britain's Maritime Heritage (1982)
Sail on the Orwell (with Roger Finch) (1982)
Beach Boats of Britain (1984)
Sail: The Surviving Tradition (1984)
East Anglian Coast and Waterways (1985)

ISBN 0 900227 79 6

Printed in England
East Anglian Magazine Publishing Limited
Duke Street, Ipswich, IP3 0AJ

The Suffolk Sandlings

Alde, Deben and Orwell country

by Robert Simper

East Anglian Magazine Publishing Limited

ACKNOWLEDGEMENTS

Some of the photographs in this book were saved by Robert G. Pratt. Future generations will be grateful to him for saving the Welton negatives. These glass plates had been left on the second floor of a chemist's shop in the Thoroughfare, Woodbridge and were to be destroyed because they had caused the floor to sag. At some risk to himself Mr. Pratt retreived them.

Geoff Cordy of Felixstowe has also been helpful with photographs and Graham Henderson of Felixstowe Ferry has generously lent some of his collection. Thanks to my wife Pearl for all her help and for typing.

Front cover:
Sailing barge Dawn moored by the Woodbridge Tide Mill in 1986

CONTENTS

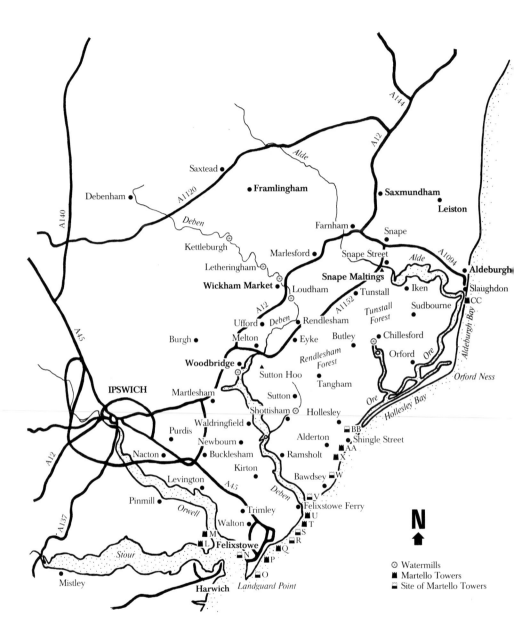

Saxtead •

Debenham •

• **Framlingham**

Alde

Saxmundham •

Leiston

A1120

A140

Deben

Farnham •

Snape •

Kettleburgh ⊙

Marlesford •

Snape Street •

Alde

A1094

Aldeburgh

Letheringham ⊙

Snape Maltings ▲

Wickham Market •

Loudham •

Tunstall •

Iken •

Slaughdon
CC

A12

A1152

Sudbourne •

Tunstall Forest

Ufford •

Deben

Rendlesham •

Chillesford ⊙ •

Burgh •

Melton •

Eyke •

Butley •

Orford •

Ore

Rendlesham Forest

Woodbridge • ⊙

▲

Sutton Hoo

Tangham •

Ore

Orford Ness

IPSWICH

Martlesham •

Sutton •

Shottisham ⊙

Hollesley •

Hollesley Bay

Aldeburgh Bay

Waldringfield •

Alderton •

BB ◼

A12

Purdis •

Newbourn •

Shingle Street •

AA ◼

Nacton •

Bucklesham •

Ramsholt •

X ◼

Kirton •

A45

Bawdsey •

W ◼

Levington •

Deben

V ◼

Pinmill •

Orwell

Felixstowe Ferry

U ◼

Walton •

• Trimley

T ◼

A137

M ◼

S ◼

Stour

L ◼

R ◼

Felixstowe

Q ◼

N ◼

P ◼

Mistley •

O ◼

N

Harwich

Landguard Point

⊙ Watermills
◼ Martello Towers
▬ Site of Martello Towers

A144

A12

A45

INTRODUCTION

After *Woodbridge & Beyond* first appeared in 1972 it became an established local favourite and was reprinted five times, but another well liked local history *Over Snape Bridge* has long been out of print. Now these two titles have been partly combined and added to to produce the history of the south eastern corner of Suffolk. Of course the history of the Woodbridge, Felixstowe, Orford, Snape and surrounding villages remains the same, but it has been retold in a different way and brought up to date.

We catch a glimpse of the Saxon Kingdom of East Anglia. The area of the ship burial at Sutton Hoo gave vital evidence of the emerging English nation. From the nineteenth century we see some of the more colourful personalities of East Suffolk and they are brought back to life in this book. We meet Edward FitzGerald whose schooner *Scandal* was named, he claimed, after the chief product of Woodbridge; the poet Bernard Barton who said he had 'Little more locomotion than a cabbage', Thomas Churchyard, the lawyer who preferred to be a painter, the irascible Colonel Tomline whose huge schemes never quite worked but somehow created Felixstowe, Sir Cuthbert Quilter whose 'splendid protest against taxation made not the slightest difference to the course of British political history', Amos Clark who claimed to have pulled down eighty Suffolk wind and watermills in his search for seasoned oak for putting on the face of mock Tudor houses.

We see how the countryside was dominated by landowners and worked by tenant farmers and whole armies of farm workers. When every tide saw sailing barges coming into the rivers to load cargoes at lonely riverside wharves. Of the long forgotten coprolite boom and the sudden and unexpected growth of the port of Felixstowe.

We see the port of Woodbridge die and the rise of boatbuilding to take the place of trade. The quiet villages where farming has for centuries been the backbone of local life have braced themselves to accept tourism. The Deben and Snape Maltings have been discovered and this book shows why.

CHAPTER ONE

SHAPING THE SANDLINGS

The south east corner of Suffolk is a country of contrast. On some maps the area between the Rivers Orwell and Alde is marked as The Sandlings, a good description of this light sandy land although it is never used in every day speech, only local literature. This is an area different from the rest of Suffolk, it is a land of open skies where the sea and salt water are never far away. In amongst the farmland, heath and forest are sprawling villages with names which suggest Saxon origins. The places which have grown into towns are all very different. Woodbridge, now a busy popular place thanks to the wealth from the service industries in the Ipswich area, still retains the atmosphere of a country market town. Orford seems to be a sleepy but extremely attractive place dreaming of its medieval importance. Much of Felixstowe is like a neat Victorian suburb of a big city. In fact it is a suburb because in its short existence Felixstowe has always depended on its road and rail links with the large urban centres. The character and shape of the towns and villages of The Sandlings are a result of long centuries of human activities.

The Romans settled in the area, but not in any great numbers, they were at Walton near Felixstowe and also at Trimley, Martlesham, Sutton and Iken. The towns and country villas along the East Anglian coast were subject to raids from Saxon pirates to such an extent that the Romans built a chain of forts to protect it. The exact location of one of these forts of the Saxon Shore has always been a mystery but a possible site is Walton Castle which is now out under the sea off the Dip at Felixstowe. As a child, just after World War II, I can remember seeing people swimming out at very low tide and sitting on the remains of Walton Castle. However, the exact origin of this fortification guarding the Deben entrance has never been established in spite of some work by underwater archaeologists.

About 450 AD the Roman Empire was crumbling at such a rate that the troops were withdrawn from the province of Britain. The Angles and Saxon people from north Germany appear to have already been raiding East Anglia and then started to arrive and settle. The north German coastal area around the Rivers Weser and Elbe is a flat land of sandy soil which even now has a poor agricultural return. In the Dark Ages, long before the massive modern sea walls were constructed, it must also have been liable to flooding from the sea. In fact the whole European coast between France and Denmark was having problems with sea encroachment. Much of the modern nation of the Netherlands was submerged by the North Sea some time during the Dark Ages.

England with its highly fertile land and a political vacuum created by the departing Roman troops was the promised land to tribal people on the other side of the North Sea. The Saxons must have found the south eastern corner of Suffolk very similar to the land they had left behind, certainly they appear to have moved in large numbers. They probably just settled in the empty land around the Britons. Just inland from Felixstowe is a place named Walton, which means 'farm of the Britons', this indicates that native Celtic people were living here after Saxons settled around them. Other place names in this area of the Felixstowe peninsula are of great antiquity and the intensity of crop marks picked out by aerial photography suggest that areas around Trimley, Kirton, Bucklesham and Levington had a large population. The early subsistence farmers found the light, sandy soils easier to work with primitive ploughs than the heavyland of High Suffolk, inland.

The Saxons were shadowy people, there is plenty of evidence that they became well established in the Woodbridge coastal area, but there are very few hard facts about the people themselves and the kind of lives that they led. There is no doubt, however, that when the Anglo Saxons came from the European mainland they brought a pagan religion with them. Later the Christians supressed most of the knowledge of these beliefs but they probably involved worship of the war god Woden and the goddess Frig. They must also have believed that goods placed in a grave would be transported to the 'after world' for the use of the dead person. In the Sandlings area two Saxon cemeteries have been revealed complete with ship burials.

In 1862 three local archaeologists decided to excavate some barrows beside the main road to Aldeburgh, just past Snape Church, and discovered a ship burial. The double ended clinker ship was about 48ft long but the only object of any importance found in it was a gold

Excavations of the Anglo-Saxon ship burial in Mound One at Sutton Hoo in 1939.

ring of about 550 AD. The ring was unique to pagan Anglo Saxon England and the burial was no doubt carried out for someone of considerable importance.

There were other mounds at the Snape Anglo Saxon cemetery, but erosion over the decades has now levelled the ground. The ship burial at Snape is thought to date from 600-650 AD in the Middle Saxon period. This discovery was more or less forgotten until the tremendous find at Sutton Hoo just before World War II.

There are probably nineteen burial mounds at Sutton Hoo and in 1938 these were overgrown with 'brakes' (bracken) standing isolated on the edge of Sutton Walks over looking the River Deben. Mrs Edith Pretty J.P., owner of the Sutton Hoo Estate was intrigued to know what lay in these mounds. The Ipswich Museum recommended that Mrs Pretty should employ Basil Brown of Rickinghall, a local man with a flair for archaeology, to excavate these mounds. He found the remains of a boat in Mound Two and that summer's dig gave him some indication of the type of problems he would meet when he tackled the largest Mound One.

In 1939 Brown and his two helpers, Mrs Pretty's gardener and handyman, started on Mound One and almost at once began to uncover a very large ship. That summer revealed the most exciting find ever made in British archaeology. There were traces of a huge double ended clinker ship about 89ft long, an amazing discovery in itself, but even more exciting was the treasure of sword, traces of clothes and every personal item needed by a great chief which had been left in what was once a burial chamber hung with tapestry. The ship and its treasure had been buried there for a person of very great stature to take into the pagan 'after world'. The archaeologists took silver plate and golden objects from the acidic, sandy soil which were still in perfect order after 1300 years of being buried. Most of the important finds from the Sutton Hoo ship burial are now to be seen in a fine display in the British Museum, London. Amongst over 200 objects retrieved from Mound One at Sutton Hoo, one rather obvious item was missing, there was no positive sign of a body. It is now assumed that it was completely destroyed by the acid soil.

Most of the Sutton Hoo mounds have been dug into at some time by robbers, but by a wonderful stroke of luck Mound One escaped this disaster because one end of the mound had been removed at some stage. When robbers dug in the centre, they were in fact in the wrong place for the centre of the original mound. World War II prevented any further excavation of Sutton Hoo, in fact the whole of Sutton Walks, then open heathland, was given over to an army combat training ground.

The Sutton Hoo treasure, which includes objects made all over Europe, has been dated from about 625 AD. There has been no real way of identifying who this burial was made for, but since the Wuffingas, the Royal house of the kings of East Anglia, are recorded as having their Royal Hall at Rendlesham, four miles further up the Deben Valley, the logical conclusion is that this was their burial ground. Of all the kings of East Anglia, the most obvious candidate for the burial is Raedwald, the most powerful of the East Anglian kings and the only one to reach the position of High King over all the other Saxon kingdoms in England.

It has been revealed, after re-examining the whole Sutton Hoo ship burial that there was a space in the burial chamber where a body could have laid, also laboratory tests of the soil from that area suggest that a body had been buried. The original excavator's notes were re-read and these revealed that iron coffin fittings were also found. The indication is that King Raedwald was buried in all his splendour and with the full ritual and feasting of a great pagan Saxon king, and around him in other mounds may have been buried the lesser members of the East

Martin Carver explains the excavation of Mound Two at Sutton Hoo in front of the BBC camera team, 1985.

Anglian Royal family.

Mound One was re-excavated by the British Museum in the 1960's but they found nothing to prove or disprove this theory. In 1984 the Birmingham Field Archaeology Unit, led by Martin Carver, started an extremely detailed excavation of the site. They found that there was a large cemetery for the common folk stretching back over about ten acres. In 1985 Martin Carver and his team were surprised at the variety of ways the Saxons were buried; one man even appeared to be buried with his plough.

The Sutton Hoo Saxon burials seem to suggest a society in the midst of great social changes at a period when they were changing from the pagan religion to Christianity. The Christian missionaries may well have concentrated on the Sandlings because it was the centre of East Anglia.

The Saxon cemeteries at Sutton Hoo and Snape have similar features, both are on a site which might have been chosen because they were on high land overlooking the tidal rivers where there were considerable settlements in pre historic times. Sutton Hoo in the late Neolithic and early Bronze Age must have been the largest settlement in the Sandlings. These early people left burial barrows at Sutton Hoo which could have attracted the Saxons to continue to use it as their ritual centre.

Sutton Hoo ship burial appears to have taken place just before Christianity was adopted by the East Anglian king. Raedwald (599-624 AD) played it safe by having altars to Christ and to the old gods in his Rendlesham Royal Hall. The adoption of Christianity made a powerful political link with the kings while keeping to the old gods no doubt pleased Raedwald's followers. When Sigeberht became king of East Anglia in about 635 AD he was determined to shake off the old gods and invited Felix to come from Burgundy to turn his kingdom finally to Christianity and gave up his kingship to become a monk.

When East Anglia was being attacked in about 640 AD by Mercia (now The Midlands) the East Anglian leaders needed to boost up their men's morale and to achieve this they forcibly abducted the saintly Sigeberht to lead them into battle against the pagan King Penda of Mercia. The monk-king Sigeberht refused to carry a sword and went into battle with a 'wand' or staff. This peaceful force gesture was wasted on the aggressive Mercians and Sigeberht was killed leaving East Anglia to become one of the lesser English Kingdoms.

East Anglia seems to have remained a Christian kingdom and was constantly trying to win allies among other kingdoms in its struggle against Mercia. In about 660 AD the king of the East Saxons was baptized Christian at the Wuffings Royal Hall at Rendlesham. The upper Deben Valley seems to have remained the heartland of Wuffing's shrinking kingdom, the Royal Hall would probably have looked like a huge wooden thatched barn, but its exact site has not yet been positively identified. An account in 1722 claimed that an ancient crown was found at Rendlesham, but more positive proof of Saxon presence was the finding, in 1837, of a cremation cemetery in glebe land to the north of the parish church of St Gregory. Since this church is dedicated to the pope who sent missionaries to England to win back the Angles to the Christian faith, it is assumed that there was a very ancient church here. John Newman, who has done much of the field walking for the Kingdom of East Anglia Survey, found Saxon pottery on a large site area of about 40 acres near St Gregory's. Within this area, on the edge of high land is Naunton Hall and it is possible that the house, garden or farm buildings might have been built over the Wuffing's Royal Hall.

Rendlesham appears to be the largest early Saxon settlement, but the survey has discovered that Sutton church is surrounded by a Saxon settlement of about 17 acres and the vanished Saxon village of Wilford was located. The church at Iken is dedicated to St Botolph, a Saxon monk who retired to live in a monastery on a marshland island in 654 AD. This again would have been just a simple timber building which was fairly certainly near the present Iken church.

The early Saxon settlements like Sutton Hoo, Rendlesham, Boyton and Barrow Hill are all sited near rivers for easy transport by boat. Barrow Hill beside the Butley River was then an island linked to the mainland by a causeway. It was settled between about 650-840 AD and most of the burials there appear to have been male suggesting an army camp or monastery but it was probably abandoned about the time the Danish Vikings started raiding the coast.

The last King of East Anglia was Edmund who was caught and then tortured to death by the pagan Danes. The Christians later turned Edmund into a martyr saint but the exact location of his terrible death has never been established. One version is that the Danes landed at Orford in 869 AD and hunted down and killed Edmund in Sutton.

In the turmoil of the Danes over-running and then settling in eastern England virtually all trace of the Wuffings kingdom vanished. Only some of the place names around the top of the River Deben give a possible haunting memory of the East Anglian kings. Ufford seems to have been the ford of the Saxon Uffa or Wuffa, while Kingston, on the southern edge of Woodbridge was literally the King's farm, but which king? This was a royal manor and in about 970 AD the West Saxon King Edgar gave this and the Melton Manor to Ely Abbey. Could this have been the last of the royal land left over from the Wuffings of the previous century?

The Deben is surrounded with places and field names with tantalizing suggestions of pagan and Saxon origins, but very little hard evidence. The very name Deben might give a clue as to why the Wuffings made their base here. The Deben was the Deep One, probably compared to the Orwell and the then separate rivers of Alde, Ore and Butley, but today the Orwell is far deeper. However, Harwich Harbour and the Orwell are man made to the present depth because of about 150 years of continual dredging. When the Anglo-Saxons and

Danes were here the Deben was a larger river and might well have been the Deep One of the Suffolk estuaries.

The Saxons certainly regarded a boat as being a major form of transport and an easily navigable river was a great advantage. Just about all Saxon settlements between 400–700 AD are beside rivers. The rivers and sea were also the way raiding Danish Vikings came so the Anglo Saxons then moved inland. Round church towers are usually believed to have been built as Saxon watch towers and it is just possible that the one at Ramsholt might have originally been built in the 900's AD so that the entrance of the Deben some four miles away could be watched.

The Danes were regularly raiding the coast by the ninth century and their most spectacular intrusion was the capture and sacking of Ipswich in 870 AD. Ipswich was by then the largest and most prosperous port on the coast and continued to grow as it became the administrative centre of Suffolk. In the medieval period, however, much of the power in this part of the country was centred on Walton near Felixstowe because Hugh Bigod, Earl of Norfolk built Walton Castle in the corner of the Roman fort there. The Bigods had land throughout Suffolk and Norfolk and virtually controlled the region through their castles at Bungay, Framlingham and Walton. It was to re-establish royal authority in East Anglia that King Henry II had Orford Castle built in 1165–75. It could be supplied by sea from London and the king's forces did not have to pass through the country held by the Bigods. Eventually Walton Castle fell into royal hands and it was Henry II who ordered it to be pulled down to make certain that the Bigods did not become a threat again.

Walton Manor, built after the castle was destroyed, remained an important royal manor and in 1338 when Edward III was fighting to try and regain control of northern France he stayed here while assembling a war fleet. The port for the royal manor of Walton was Goseford which was a large creek leading from the Deben just above Felixstowe Ferry. There was never a town at Goseford, just a place where ships discharged and no trace of it now remains. It must have been somewhere on the Kingsfleet, a drainage ditch now closed from the Deben which runs up behind Walton and Felixstowe. In Suffolk, fleet means shallow and Kingsfleet was simply the shallow creek used by the kings. In 1346 Goseford sent 13 ships and 303 mariners to fight with Edward III at the siege of Calais and this king later granted Goseford men the right to supply Calais with beer and provisions.

Goseford was doomed as a port inspite of its royal support because it was too near the coast and did not have a hinterland to service. Woodbridge replaced it as the market town of the Sandlings and had a further advantage in being able to draw on the rich agricultural land and timber supply of heavyland Suffolk around Framlingham. There is no record of there being a wooden bridge over the Deben, some believe that the name Woodbridge is a corruption of Woden burgh from the far off pagan Saxon days, of the cult of Woden. Others believe the wooden bridge was spanned over Steyning Brook near Drybridge Hill, certainly the original town was up near the Market Hill.

As the manorial system developed, the wood bridge settlement became a series of small manors centred on the Market Hill. This had by then become a common meeting place. The Domesday Book mentions the original Parish Church of St Mary's. In the 12th century Ernaldus Rufus founded a small Augustinian (black) Canons Priory near the present site of Woodbridge Abbey House. This religious body acquired market rights for the little town.

At the same time as the market became established, Woodbridge began to flourish as a port. Products from the villages around were shipped out. This activity was controlled by merchants and the town began to expand. Salt making was an occupation of some importance and other crafts which have long since died out included wool combing and hat and rope making.

All this brought modest wealth to the people of the town. In the second half of the 15th century the merchants rebuilt the parish church of St Mary in fine perpendicular style with a western tower of cut flints with freestone dressing. Later, in Cromwellian times, Dowsing and his soldiers visited the church with the aim of removing what they considered to be idols. These gentlemen did a great deal of damage to the churches in the Eastern Counties and, at Woodbridge, they mutilated the font. To those who were fond of church architecture, Dowsing was a scoundrel, but the majority of Woodbridge people at that time approved. In an area noted for its Nonconformists, the town was very much a Puritan stronghold. The town's tradesmen and craftsmen took no part in the established church and actively disliked anything faintly connected with the High Church.

Thomas Seckford was a colourful Elizabethan who managed to

make his name well remembered in the town. When the priory was suppressed early in the 16th century, its land passed into the hands of his family. Seckford became a lawyer and held important official positions at the Court of Queen Elizabeth. He built Seckford Hall, which is just outside the town, in about 1560, but since this was an enlightened age he devoted most of his wealth towards helping others who were less fortunate. At the time the seat of justice was transferred from Melton to Woodbridge, Seckford built the lovely red brick Shire Hall which stands in the middle of the Market Hill, in 1570. This elegant building with Dutch Gables still served as the Sessions Hall and in the days when Woodbridge was a market town was also used as the Corn Exchange. The Shire Hall was restored in 1884 when it was briefly used as a fire station before it changed again to be the Petty Sessions Court. It was the centre of local justice for over four centuries before 1886 when the court was moved to Ipswich.

Thomas Seckford's greatest achievement was the setting up of the Seckford Hospital which housed 26 aged single men. The Seckford Charities derived their revenues from an estate in Clerkwell, London and from four streets in Woodbridge. All of these were left to the Charities by Seckford after his death in 1587. By 1861 the income from the Seckford charities was large enough to build the Seckford Almshouse in Seckford Street. The original hospital was no longer sufficient for the town's needs. Later, in 1886, the Seckford Dispensary was built and it wasn't until the 1930's that this petered out through lack of funds.

Thomas Seckford must have found his brother something of an embarrassment for the town's benefactor could not have been pleased with the knowledge that his brother Henry was a fairly successful pirate. There is no record of Henry Seckford giving money to the poor. Perhaps he financed a few drinking sprees in the town's ale houses after returning from his voyages. Once when he was master of the *Lyon* he seized the Spanish merchantman *Bonaventure* and took her into a South Coast port where he sold her cargo of wools, saffron and bacon. Such actions against the Spanish were favoured by Queen Elizabeth I and perhaps Thomas Secford's influence at court helped to smooth out any difficulties. In 1592, however, Henry suffered a financial setback when he was fined £12,000 for taking a Venetian ship 'by mistake'.

Woodbridge still largely retains its Tudor character. Its personality

Traffic direction man at the Cross Corner, Woodbridge about 1900.

is not so much in any particularly beautiful building, but in the whole homely appeal of its narrow streets which have charm that could not have been created artificially. Many of the original Tudor houses had fronts altered at a later period and in more recent years some have been swept away all together.

In the early stage-coach days, the London-Yarmouth highway went up to the Market Hill and down the other side, but in the eighteenth century the Thoroughfare became the main route. This had been a residential street, but developed into the business area in between the port and the market and became the real centre of the town.

The 17th century saw the town reach the zenith of its importance as a port. Also shipbuilding was at its peak. The port was rivalling Ipswich and turning out men-of-war for the navy. The town depended so much on shipping that after the railway went through in 1859 the population dropped dramatically. The town's growth was stunted and it was left just a quiet country backwater until light industries sprang up in the 1930's.

The Suffolk coast had always been a possible place for an invasion from Europe during time of war. A garrison was first established at Woodbridge in 1750, but it was not until the Napoleonic wars that large bodies of troops were stationed here. In 1803 barracks covering 56 acres were put up on Drybridge Hill. These were to accommodate 700 cavalrymen and 4,000 infantrymen. In 1805 the 21st Light Dragoons were here. A large number of Georgian houses were built for the officers and it was probably because of them that a small theatre was erected. This seems to have given its audiences a fairly simple diet of light comedies. However, the townspeople were not impressed and complained that the theatre was 'old fashioned'. In fact the people of the peaceful country market town loathed the task of quartering the red coats. The chief amusement of the healthy young soldiers was getting drunk and having a good scrap, a habit which must have placed severe strain on the tempers of the regular chapel attenders. The defeat of Napoleon was greeted with enthusiasm not because it meant the end of a tyrant, but because soldiers were no longer needed in Suffolk. The barracks were pulled down in 1815.

The 19th century saw a little group of cultured men living in Woodbridge, most of whom are now forgotten outside their home town. The first of these was Bernard Barton (1784–1849). This quiet Quaker was a clerk at Alexanders Bank (now Barclays) who wrote poems in his spare time. These poems achieved national fame and in 1845 Bernard Barton dined with the Prime Minister, Sir Robert Peel, at Whitehall. The following year he was granted a special pension by Queen Victoria.

Barton had many literary friends, but by far the closest was Edward FitzGerald (1809-1883). Born at Bredfield House, 'Old Fitz' was third son of John Purcell, who married his cousin Mary FitzGerald. After her father's death, the Purcell's legally adopted the FitzGerald name and arms. Also the great wealth that went with them. As well as property in Ireland, other estates they owned were Bredfield House, Boulge Hall, Wherstead Park and Nazeby.

FitzGerald lived the life of a gentleman. He moved about a great deal, but his first home was Boulge Cottage, then for 13 years he lodged over the shop of Berry the gun maker, on the Market Hill. Finally he had the Little Grange built to his own plans, but still preferred his humble rooms over the gun maker's shop. He did not move

The Waller family of Waldringfield and friends on a boating expedition about 1885.
(Source: Waller Collection)

Mrs Berry and her pony and trap at Woodbridge about 1905 (Source: G. F. Cordy)

until he had a disagreement with his landlord.

One of FitzGerald's great interests was literature and he was particularly keen on translating the classics. As a boy he had been filled with the romance of The East, by meeting Major Moor of Bealings House. This retired officer of The East India Company studied Suffolk words and archaeology. FitzGerald never visited the East, but began passing away the time translating the works of a medieval Persian poet Omar Khayyam. These translations gained a great deal from FitzGerald's own poetic ability. His friends were interested in them and for their benefit he had a few printed and published in small paper cover editions. Those who read the 'Rubaiyat of Omar Khayyam' were struck by its originality.

After Barton's death, FitzGerald married his daughter Lucy. This was not a love match, the couple were middle aged and FitzGerald was beguiled into believing that this was the way to care for his old friend's daughter. Unfortunately, the lady tried to force him to conform – dress for dinner and send out visiting cards. FitzGerald hated display and the couple soon parted. He remained aloof from his surroundings and spent the rest of his life appreciating the beauty of East Anglia. He mixed only with a little group of cultured man who referred to themselves as the Wits of Woodbridge. This had consisted of Barton, The Rev. Crabbe, grandson of the Aldeburgh poet, Captain Brook of Ufford Place and the lawyer Thomas Churchyard (1798-1865).

Churchyard practised law in the local courts, but his real interest lay in painting. A capable amateur artist, his work is a poetic record of Victorian Woodbridge. Although Churchyard did a number of oils, most of his works were small watercolours dashed off at great speed as if they were studies of something to be finished later. He bought and copied paintings by John Constable and thus developed the same style. Churchyard's art was an important link between Constable and East Anglian painting in the 19th century. Had Churchyard's heart been in his profession he would have grasped high honours and the financial rewards that went with them. But he had the overwhelming desire to paint. In 1832 his affairs collapsed and there was a sale of his belongings. Then married with five children, he left the district for a time, possibly to try his luck in London. However, he returned and lived in Seckford Street (then Well Street) and for the last 30 years of his life he lived in Cumberland Street.

Churchyard used his ability and knowledge of the law to defend the under dog. He was something of a champion of the poor and particularly disliked the 'game preservers' and their head keepers. He delighted in seeing the local poachers walk down the Shire Hall steps after their cases had been dismissed. But fate played a cruel trick on this habit. The agent of the Marquis of Hertford, one of the largest game preservers in the district, persuaded his employer to pay Churchyard a retainer as the prosecuting solicitor in all game cases. Churchyard's finances were such that he was unable to turn this offer down. It was a sad blow for the poachers.

Perhaps Churchyard was something of a poacher himself. Certainly he enjoyed a day out with a gun and dog, rough shooting. On one occasion he took his favourite retriever into the shop of the Quaker Confectioner Barritt. Unbeknown to Churchyard the dog ate a number of sausage rolls. A few days later Barritt was standing in his shop doorway when Churchyard came walking down the street. Barritt told him that a dog had eaten some of his sausage rolls.

"Oh," said Churchyard, "you can recover against the owner of the dog."

"Then hand over eighteen pence," cried the Quaker. "It was your dog."

"Very well," said the quick witted lawyer, "I charge you six and eightpence for advice and the balance due to me is five and twopence."

CHAPTER TWO

UP TO SNAPE BRIDGE

The Suffolk coast could be called the Invasion Coast. The Saxons and
Danish Vikings raided and settled here, but later continental invaders
found their way barred. The coast is littered with fortifications constructed to keep out Napoleon, the Kaiser and Hitler, and the defences
of the Cold War are still much in evidence. Another form of invasion
came from the sea itself which is steadily gnawing away at the soft
sandy land. More recently the coast has been subject to increasing
preasure from tourism and rising residential population.

The coastal hamlet of Shingle Street seems to have seen more than
its fair share of these forms of invasion. Shingle Street grew up when
the Martello Tower was built in 1812 as part of a coastal chain built to
keep Napoleon out. The single storey cottages on the shingle were
built largely of driftwood which was in great supply in an age when
every gale saw sailing ships wrecked on Orfordness. Shingle Street
was cut off from the rest of the world except for a track along the beach
to Bawdsey and it became part of that parish. Later a road was built
across the Oxley Marshes linking it with Hollesley so that at least it was
easier for fresh water to be brought in daily by horse and cart.

Most of the Shingle Street men picked up a living by fishing, salvaging and pilotage into the River Ore or whatever else came along.
Holiday homes started here in about 1895 when the red brick German
Ocean Mansion was built. This house soon lost its original name when
the Kaiser attempted to dominate Europe and the German Ocean had
its name changed to the North Sea.

A far earlier invasion had caused the Saxons to abandon their settlement on Barrow Hill, Butley. The Saxons had buried their chiefs at
Snape and must have had settlements at the head of this long winding
estuary because eight Saxon ovens have been found here. The
medieval village of Snape was in the now open fields to the north of the
Parish Church and there was a Benedictine Priory founded in 1155
near the Saxon ship burial mound.

The great religious houses controlled most of the income from the

Sandlings in the medieval period. Snape Priory owned the open sheep walks to the north east and the fishing rights of the sea off Aldeburgh. The Priory's wealth allowed it to build on a grand scale. A timber framed barn built by the Priory in about 1235 is still standing and is still in use. A wooden building of good timber will last longer than many forms of construction providing it is kept dry. In the case of the barn at Snape it has had some 750 years of continual use.

Butley Abbey Farm also has a farm building which dates back to medieval religious orders. The building has 4ft thick stone walls and has recently had an animal food mixing plant in it, but it was monks cells. The farm has a misleading name because it was an Augustinian order which started the Priory here in 1171. The present Butley Priory is in fact only the gatehouse to a now vanished huge complex of buildings and was converted to a private house in the 1930's by a retired public school headmaster.

Ely Abbey owned a great deal of land in the Orford area and there is still an Ely Hill in Boyton. Butley Priory was responsible for reclaiming many of the marshes around the Butley River and they also claimed ownership of the river bed, whereby in most estuaries the Crown owns everything below the high tide mark. When Butley Priory set out to reclaim the Gedgrave Marshes the Orford men tried, by active protest, to stop it, but the all powerful Priory still reclaimed them,no doubt, for sheep grazing, as wool was the backbone of this area's wealth in the medieval period. In 1583 the tide was still flooding Buckanay Marshes between Shingle Street and Alderton and it was probably the land hungry Elizabethans who were responsible for another burst of walling marshes after this.

Butley Priory also purchased Staverton Park and hunting guests were entertained here. This piece of ancient woodland was a medieval deer park created before 1260 by throwing up an earth bank to enpark about 370 acres. In the medieval period much of the remaining forest the Sandlings was cleared for farming, but Staverton remained untouched behind its earth banks. In 1528 the Queen of France picnicked under the oaks in Staverton while 'hunting of foxes'. After the dissolutionment of the monasteries, Staverton passed through the ownership of several great land owners, but early in this century the grazing of sheep in the park stopped. The Park and the Thicks, next to the road, remain a unique area of oak and hollies. The tallest holly tree in Britain is here, the Guinness Book of Records gives a height of 73ft

The anti-aircraft gun tower on the Rough Sands off Bawdsey was created during World War II and later claimed by Roy Bates as an 'independent state', Sealand.

9in. There are no mentions of hollies before 1819 but they may have been there as both pagan and Christian ceremonies used them and this may have prompted their preservation.

Staverton Park survived World War II, but only just. Along with the Battle Schools at Iken, Sudbourne, Sutton Walks and Shingle Street this was a military training centre. Staverton was used for tank exercises and the park was damaged further by a German and British aircraft crashing and setting light to a large area. Also trees were moved for a flight path for Bentwater's Aerodrome.

Deer were kept as decoration in Campsea Ash Park and some seem to have escaped during the war and established wild herds. In the 1950's fallow deer from the forestry reappeared in Staverton and in 1982 the owner, farmer and conservationist Jack Kemball created a deer park by enclosing the south end of Staverton. Time has done a full circle for once more, under the 400 year old oaks, deer are grazing, just as they had done in medieval Staverton.

In the medieval period Staverton was a valuable asset for hunting, but the real wealth of the Sandlings came from the sheep which roamed on the open walks. These sheep walks were abandoned in the nineteenth century and then grew over as open heath and were used by great estate owners for shooting. The great landowners from Rendlesham Hall, Ash High House, Sudbourne Hall, Bawdsey Manor and Orwell Park controlled most of the Sandlings and started tree planting to provide game cover. Lord Rendlesham made a serious attempt at planting up Tangham Walks which were destroyed by fire, but in 1920 this was sold to the newly formed Forestry Commission. The Commission planted up the 7,022 acres to form Rendlesham and Tunstall Forests and buried the hamlet of Tangham in the cold sea of evergreen trees, all to feed the coal mines with pit props.

Sheep were once the 'golden hooves' of the Sandlings, but by 1985 there were only three large flocks between the Orwell and the Alde. Even dairy herds are almost extinct as intensive arable agriculture looked to be the most likely way to survive the agricultural recession. The grazing marshes behind the river walls were turned into wheat land after the East Coast Flood of 1953 when Government pressure encouraged farmers to plough land rather than return it to grass. Before that, marsh land had been summer grazing for sheep and cattle. In the eighteenth century cattle were walked down from Scotland to be fattened in East Anglia for the London market. In the railway age it was mostly Irish cattle which came to the marshes around the Sandling estuaries. Even Havergate Island, that lonely patch of marsh in the River Ore, had a house for the marshman and his family who looked after the cattle. These beasts were walked down the river wall from Orford and swum across the Gull to Havergate, although at one time there was a huge punt for taking cattle across to King's and Lantern marshes on Orfordness. Sadly all the sheep here in 1953 were drowned in the flood.

On the opposite side of Havergate Island, in the main channel of Narrows, there was once an oyster fishery. Orford appeared as a town with Corporation status because of the medieval wool trade and had managed to get the fishing rights over the River Ore. In about 1788 there was a very hard frost which killed most of the Essex oysters so smacks from Brightlingsea came to the River Ore and tried to establish that it was a free fishery. There was a series of legal disputes between the Essexmen and the men of Orford which came to a head in 1791 when 52 Essex smacks arrived in force to dredge in the Ore. The Orford men came down in force to the lower end of Havergate where they attempted to board an Essex smack, but the Orford boat was sunk. Inspite of feelings running high, the Orford men managed to confiscate some oyster dredges. The matter was finally settled in court where Orford Town upheld its right to the River Ore.

In 1883 Orford lost its mayor and its ancient status as a borough, but the river rights remained in the Town Trust. The oyster fishery faded out in the 1920's and after World War II, when Richard Pinney went to live at Gedgrave, he noticed many old oyster shells beside the Butley River. In search of a way to earn a living in this lonely place, he established an oyster cultivation in the Butley River. The next step was to open the unique Butley-Orford Oysterage Restaurant, run by Mrs Pinney, and this was able to take the advantage of the rising tide of tourists. William Pinney took over the fishery side from his father, but began to do more sea fishing with a high speed power boat from Butley River. When he switched to the decked *Nichola Dawn,* operating from Orford Quay, he was able to stay at sea longer, usually three tides when working long lines for cod off the coast.

In the winter other boats came in and worked from Orford, but it has never been a great fishing centre. The quay had regular sailing barge traffic until the 1920's but this was to the end of a causeway down from the market place. The medieval ships loaded wool in a creek beside this causeway on the opposite side to *The Jolly Sailor.* Now the marsh stretches away to the north through a countryside still haunted by the 'bobbing lights'. There was an east coast legend that a kind of marsh ghost appeared at night and could do harm to anyone who approached the dancing lights. In fact this was a story put about by eighteenth century sumugglers to discourage local people from taking too close an interest in their nocturnal activities. In this century faint memories of smugglers gangs were still alive and old people said that the cellars in farmhouses in Boyton and Hollesley were built for hiding contraband. The Dumb Boy's Cottage in Hollesley is said to have got its name because a dumb man who lived there was employed by the smugglers because he could not give their secrets away.

At some indefinable spot above Orford, the River Ore changes its name to the River Alde. The head of the Alde is dominated by the great Snape Maltings which is one of the few industrial buildings which fits in with its rural surroundings. The bridge over the Alde is linked to Snape along a road which was originally a man-made causeway. The exact date of the first bridge is not known, but over the centuries it was the subject of endless local disputes over whose responsibility it was to maintain it. In 1347 the landowner had to repair it while in 1492 Aldeburgh and Orford were wanting each other to be responsible for the bridge. By 1571 Snape was supposed to repair one end and Tunstall the other. In about 1802 a brick hump back bridge was built and this lasted until 1960 when the present more sensible, but less attractive bridge was built.

As a crossing point of the river, Snape has long been a focal point in the area. Between 1727-1842 there was an annual horse race over seven miles which was held on the Snape Race Course. Even older was the Dunningworth Horse Fair, held in front of Dunningworth Hall Farm near Snape Maltings. This sale of Suffolk Punch cart horses took its name from the lost Domesday village of Dunningworth.

At the beginning of the nineteenth century Osborne & Fennell ran a corn & coal business at Snape Bridge. There was a quay here with a few wooden sheds and a cottage, but this was changed when Newson Garrett bought the business in 1840. He began making malt and shipping it to London. Snape was ideal for a maltings because one of the few crops that would grow on the light land in the Sandlings was barley suitable for malt. The barley was turned into malt in the winter and shipped by sailing barges to the Thames breweries. The more beer the Londoners drank, the more need there was for malt and at intervals between 1846-95 bricklayers and carpenters were summoned to Snape to add another building on to the Maltings. To Garrett, Snape Maltings was more than just an industrial building for making money, the front of the maltings, with its stylish 1859 arch, shows that he intended it to be a personal status symbol. East Anglia is dotted with maltings, but none have as picturesque appearance as the one beside Snape Bridge.

Newson Garrett died aged 81 in 1893 after dominating affairs around the River Alde for most of the Victorian era. The very last malt house, now rebuilt as the concert hall, was known as the 'new house' to the end of its working days. This was put up after Garrett's death when his son, George was managing the maltings. By that time the maltings had about 7 acres of floor space and employed about 30 men. The business continued to grow a little and the final building, a grain store built in the same style, was not put up until 1952.

Local barley could not support this huge complex so cheaper imported barley was brought in by sailing barges from London Docks.

The front of Snape Maltings in 1966.

Coal and coke for the malt drying kilns came by barge too but there was also a branch railway line with a speed limit of 15 mph which was built to link Snape with Saxmundham and provide a wider distribution for Snape's different brands of malt.

World War II stopped the barge traffic and the tiny branch line, only just over a mile long, closed in 1960. After this Snape Maltings was fed by lorries but by this time Snape Maltings had become thoroughly outdated and was a charming piece of Victorian enterprise which was removed in every sense from modern industrial Britain. When S. Swonnell & Son, who had amalgamated with Garretts in 1919, went into voluntary liquidation in 1965 and the Snape Maltings closed down there were then forty-two men working at this floor maltings. I remember going into the building just after it had finished and seeing rows of malsters shovels and other tools standing against the wall in what is now the Tea Room. When I had come here with a lorry to deliver barley for malt there had always been a feeling that events moved slowly at Snape, but when the Maltings actually closed the vast set of empty buildings were deadly silent. That row of shovels, left so carefully on that final days work, marked the end of at least 120 years of malting at Snape.

Since it was easier to put up new maltings than adapt the low floor building at Snape, most people expected the Maltings to decay away as an industrial white elephant and then be pulled down. However, George Gooderham was convinced that the Maltings, the 'Plough & Sail' and all the houses that had given accommodation to the malsters must have some use. He purchased the Snape Maltings property and influenced by the success of Felixstowe decided to reopen it as a port with warehouse facilities.

It was then twenty-six years since the last barge had gone up the madly twisting channel past Iken Church to the quay at Snape. We went up the channel in my gaff cutter *Sea Fever* to try and discover what depth was still there. It seemed that there was enough water at high water for a barge so George Gooderham consulted Jumbo Ward, the river pilot, who said there was plenty of water there.

Jumbo Ward lived in the little cottage overlooking the river at Iken Cliff. He had a great knowledge of the upper Alde and he told us that in the old days it had often taken several days to get a loaded sailing barge up the last few reaches to the Maltings. Jumbo's grandfather 'Ducker' Ward had gone to sea in 1858 and then became skipper of Newson Garrett's ketch *Hope* Jumbo had piloted the last sailing barges up the river and when he brought the first motor barge, *Atrato* up in 1965 he mystified the young skipper by giving him instructions in sailing terms "luff up round that mark and bear away to loo'ward after that".

Jumbo regularly brought up barges after that and also the first imported cargo from Rotterdam on the 103ft, 250 ton coastal vessel *Gillation* in 1967, but it was felt that to reopen Snape properly someone had to bring back a sailing barge. To achieve this we all boarded the sailing barge *Lord Roberts* at Harwich and took the tide to the River Ore where we began to sail up between the low banks.

The *Lord Roberts* had given up carrying cargoes and instead was carrying young people on holiday voyages. As the barge swept up river she must have made an impressive sight under the cloud of brown sails.

Off Havergate Island, two birdwatchers appeared running down towards the river, with binoculars, cameras, the lot. They were clearly impressed by the sight of the sixty-six year old Maldon Stacky barge.

"Hey", drawled Jimmy, the skipper, innocently, "is this the right way to Ipswich?"

There was a long pause before the answer came back that we were in

Crescent Shipping's motor vessel Bencol at Snape Quay about 1970.

the wrong river!

By now the masts of two barges laying off Orford could be seen. We all half expected to see them break out their tops'ls and go up river in front, but we need not have worried for neither the *Millie* nor the *Remercie* showed any sign of robbing us of our glory, they stayed firmly anchored.

Just below Slaughden quay, Jumbo Ward came aboard.

"Yer'l have ter spring yer luff matee to get through the yachts."

"She's got an engine" said Jimmy, and Tony Winter dived below to start it.

It was agreed that we should motor through the yachts and then we still had three hours flood tide, to beat the rest of the way up under sail.

Off Iken Church, the narrow channel corkscrewed across a wide expanse of mud. Jimmy was at the wheel, Jumbo stood beside him. The dialogue between these two owed nothing to the twentieth century, W. W. Jacobs might have written it, Newson Garrett's skippers would have spoken it. When an American jet fighter screeched overhead, we were not in the same age.

"Wind her a-fore the next withy."

"Bout oh" sang out Jimmy, swinging the wheel. The barge fell off on the next tack.

"Let go yer bowline Peter", the heavy canvas fores'l shot across the deck.

"There's a lump here soon", said Jumbo. Almost at once one lee-board started churning up mud.

"Get it up!" ordered Jimmy. Two strong men wound the winch like mad. The mud kept on coming to the surface.

"I'll make another trip, Jumbo", Jimmy spun the wheel across once more.

"Make a fetch to the next withy and keep her just to the weather," ordered the pilot.

"Creek sailing" Jimmy Lawrence called this. He was in fact sailing into the wind in a channel barely wider than the vessel's length. A modern yacht would have been hard put to equal this performance. No other type of sailing trading vessel could have out sailed her under these conditions.

Jimmy kept just the mains'l and tops'l set, keeping the barge right up into the wind and with the help of the tide, made way forward. When he wanted to go about he ordered "up fores'l and aback it." Once the bows had come round, the fores'l was taken down.

A small yacht of about two tons kept just under the *Lord Roberts'* transom. The man at her tiller no doubt thought that if there was enough water for us, there must be for him. Just as the barge went about for the umpteenth time since Aldeburgh, the yacht went aground. The man at the tiller looked surprised and shouted to be pulled off.

"We came here to load sand," Tony remembered the old standing joke in barge circles.

"He ought to take his sails down instead of keep waving his hands in the air," said Jimmy in a very unconcerned voice.

After a lot of sweat had been lost, we rounded the last bend under Iken Hall. From now on, it was a fair wind, nothing could stop us from reaching Snape. There was very much the end-of-term spirit on board.

Another small yacht had just anchored right in the middle of the channel. We glided past, our mast and sails towering above her. The three men in the yacht looked worried, very worried.

"That's alright" said Jimmy, in his own slow way. "We'll get by me old mates, but yer want to watch out for the steamer coming up astern."

The three men stared back in blank amazement. Not only was it a long time since sailing barges had been up there, but it was just as long since the Snape river had sampled the dry humour of a sailing barge skipper.

The final reaches were easy, with only part of the tops'l set, we slowly weaved up the last half mile, touched the quay and swung round in the quiet water under the buildings, still an hour before high water.

In the late 1960's it looked as if Snape would become one of East Anglia's new boom ports, especially when a massive early warning station was built on Lantern Marshes. There were strong objections to heavy lorries going through the streets of Aldeburgh so the heavy materials were brought in by sea instead or shipped down from Snape Quay. During the winter of 1968-69 an average of 1500 tons a week was being loaded at Snape and often as many as seven barges lay at the quay.

Another page in Snape Malting's history was opened when Aldeburgh Festival took a long lease on the 'New House' part of the maltings. The Festival took place in early summer and revolved around the works of the Suffolk composer Benjamin Britten. Since Aldeburgh had no buildings large enough for a concert hall the Festival commissioned Arup Associates, who had previously designed the Sydney Opera House, Australia, to turn the New House into a concert hall, but to retain the character of the building. The original building had to be heightened, but around the entrance it was painted black, following the pattern by which traditional cottage walls were tarred in the Sandlings.

In 1967 the concert hall was officially opened by Her Majesty Queen Elizabeth II, but barely two years later Her Majesty returned to reopen it after the rebuilding from the ashes. The exact cause of the fire which destroyed the hall on the night of June 7-8, 1969 has never been fully explained, but it was thought to have been an electrical fault.

Everyone had left the hall after the first performance of the third Festival at Snape when the fire started behind the stage of the auditorium. The actual blaze was seen for miles around and so intense was the heat that the walls had no soot on them. The walls of the hall had been built of Aldeburgh brick seventy-six years before, yet apart from damaging

The burnt out concert hall at Snape Maltings on the day after the fire of 1969.

a few surface bricks they had stood the fire. In the rebuilding, Arup
Associates did not simply pull out the plans from the drawer and begin
again. Instead they re-thought the whole building on the basis of suggestions put forward in the Aldeburgh Festival questionnaire.

The concert hall was rebuilt in a year and reopened for the next Festival. Benjamin Britten's lifelong friend, the opera singer Peter Pears
said of the concert hall "It was built on a shoestring but the second time
the shoestring is a little stronger." A few years later the shoestring took
on further strength and the concert hall spread into the adjoining
building. Later on classical music took over the barley store at the end
of the New House complex when it became the Britten Pears School
for Advanced Music Studies. Courses here were started in 1972, mostly for young singers and string players.

Many more casual visitors came to Snape just to look at the concert
hall than ever heard a performance and this was the start of another
role for Snape Maltings as a tourist attraction. This was already well

under way when George and Sue Gooderham opened the Snape Craft Shop in 1971. In fact the whole district was growing as a tourist area and Snape followed the example of Aldringham Craft Market in, to begin with, selling hand made goods produced locally.

The creation of the concert hall in the traditional building at Snape Maltings by Aldeburgh Festival has had a profound effect on the architecture in East Suffolk and it is possible that it even contributed to a national change of thinking. In the fifties and sixties there was a tremendous amount of redevelopment in Suffolk and everything Victorian or even older was torn down without a second thought. At Snape Arup showed that old buildings could be given a new lease of life and the area was saved from being swamped by the dull urban architecture of that period.

CHAPTER THREE

THE TWO FELIXSTOWES

The nineteenth century saw a tremendous rise in the size of the population of Europe, and driven in search of space and opportunities people went out to new lands all over the world. It is easy to forget that many towns in the United States, Canada and Australia simply did not exist before the nineteenth century. It is equally easy to forget that in Britain, that same tide of growing population also created new towns, particularly seaside resorts where houses and streets mushroomed up to cover once open fields. One such new town was Felixstowe.

In 1844 Felixstowe was a village with 552 people living there. The coast of Felixstowe almost faces south and is slightly warmer than most beaches in Suffolk. This fact coupled with the interesting view from the cliff top of the shipping coming into Harwich Harbour made it a pleasant place to visit. The man who started to develop Felixstowe was John Chevallier Cobbold who built the Bath Hotel and in the 1850's was encouraging visitors to come sea bathing from the beach just to the south of Cobbold's Point. The travel links with the outside world at that time were the horse drawn coaches. The horse drawn Civility Coach which left the *Coach & Horses* at Ipswich every day at 9.30am and returned at 6.30pm charged a fare of two shillings (10p) single or three shillings (15p) return. The other way summer visitors could come was by railway to Harwich and then cross by ferry to Felixstowe.

Harwich and Dovercourt were already growing as a port and a resort owing to the railway link with Colchester. In the early 1870's the eccentric Colonel George Tomline, owner of the Orwell Park Estate and a man of considerable wealth, told Harwich that he was prepared to stand as their member of Parliament. Tomline was not at all pleased when Harwich flatly refused this offer and he became firmly convinced that Felixstowe could be developed as both a resort and a port which would take away the trade from Harwich and Dovercourt.

When Tomline got an Act before Parliament to build a railway from Ipswich to Felixstowe it was Harwich's turn to fight tooth and nail to

*In the early nineteenth century the first beach huts appeared at Felixstowe.
(Source: G. F. Cordy)*

stop the project to prevent it taking away from the Parkeston Quay plan. However, Tomline's Felixstowe Railway & Pier Company got the all important Act to build the railway line. The line ran some twelve miles from Westerfield, where it joined the Ipswich-Lowestoft line, to the Beach Station to the south of the town where Tomline believed the new resort would grow up. Even then there was considerable criticism that the five stations on the line were sited in the wrong places.

Tomline not only promoted the Felixstowe line, he was also virtually the sole owner. The men working the Felixstowe line wore the same livery as Tomline's household staff, the station master having the uniform of a butler. Even in Victorian Britain, where the rich were very rich, it was rare for one man to own a whole railway. The financial strain of the new line turned out to be even more than Tomline could afford and he had to sell it which upset him deeply as it was his favourite project. However, Tomline was already into even more schemes, building the Pier Hotel for passengers to use in his new port and the Manor House Hotel near the Beach Station.

Tomline was also into his next great scheme by forming the Felixstowe Railway & Dock Company and in 1881 Walton Creek (the remains of the old entrance to Harwich Harbour) was dammed up and work started on building the new dock. The whole enterprise cost £101,000, a vast amount of capital for one man to raise even in Victorian times. There is a story that once the money to pay the Irish labourers who were digging the dock failed to arrive and the angry workmen rioted and beseiged the surveyor in his house until the money was brought. Felixstowe tidal dock was opened for small ships in 1884 and larger ones in 1886, but it failed to become the Gateway to Europe at that time as Tomline had hoped.

Tomline's great schemes for his resort and dock did not come to much, but the town of Felixstowe started to mushroom out thanks to the railway. By 1894 it had a population of nearly 10,000 and became an Urban District Council with its own Town Hall. In 1914 it united with the ancient parish of Walton to form the present Felixstowe.

Although already a thriving resort Felixstowe received a tremendous boost when in 1891 the Empress of Germany was advised to take a holiday at Felixstowe for health reasons. She arrived with her children and a small army of servants and stayed at the Bath Hotel while the German yacht *Hohenzollern* lay at anchor offshore. In an age when royalty set the fashion, a visit by an Empress created publicity which resulted in an influx of visitors.

In the Edwardian era Felixstowe had everything a fashionable English resort required. At the foot of the Hamilton Cliff (The Duke of Hamilton had once owned most of the land around Felixstowe) was a natural spring of water which had medicinal qualities. In 1908 the Council built the Spa Pavilion for concert party entertainment and in 1904 a pier, half a mile long, was built to replace Tomline's old wooden pier. The new pier was a calling point during the summer for passenger steamers which ran from London to the East Coast resorts. Also there were river steamers which operated between Felixstowe, Harwich and Ipswich.

On a prime site on the top of the cliff the huge Felix Hotel, the ultimate in Edwardian luxury hotels, was built between 1900-1903. The Felix was staffed by Germans until World War I, a reminder that until the war Germany was considered Britain's European sister country. Felixstowe was a resort to which the titled and wealthy came regularly and the *Felixstowe Times* used to print on its front page a list

Summer visitors on the promenade near Felixstowe Spa Pavilion in the Edwardian period. (Source: G. F. Cordy)

The Felix Hotel at Felixstowe surrounded by croquet lawns. The Felix became the head office of Fisons after World War II and has now been converted to luxury flats. (Source: G. F. Cordy)

of 'top drawer' guests staying in the town.

The Felix received a royal guest in 1934 when the Prince of Wales stayed here during his visit to the Royal Show at Ipswich. Mrs Simpson also stayed here and the whole town was a hot bed of gossip about the prince, who later briefly became King Edward VIII, having a love affair with this married American lady.

My own memories of Felixstowe started as a child, just after World War II when we used to go over the Bawdsey Ferry to visit my grandmother's beach hut at the Dip. The main attraction of this stretch of beach was the tripper boat run by the Ford family. There were several other boats operating off the main Felixstowe beach running trips 'Round the Corklight'. There was a lightvessel off Felixstowe marking the Cork Sand from 1844-1975 and in calm weather the crew used to allow trippers to look round. A hat was passed around for a tip at the end of the visit.

I used to explore Felixstowe by bicycle and went on to the southern end around Landguard Marshes to find the isolated Felixstowe Dock. There were often sailing barges discharging here at Marriages Flour Mill or the Maltings and there was the added attraction of seaplanes landing in Harwich Harbour. Felixstowe Dock had become part of a defensive system when in 1904 it was the headquarters of a torpedo boat and destroyer flotilla. The next step was the construction of the Felixstowe Air Station on the south side of the Dock. This was part of a chain of seaplane bases which were in full operation by the outbreak of World War I. During World War II the dock was the base of the Royal Navy's fast light coastal craft better known as the 'Little Ships'. Since most of the crews apparently used the Pier Hotel as their drinking place it was renamed, in the spirit of the day, *The Little Ships.*

The navy and seaplane station remained prominent at Felixstowe Dock until the end of the 1940's but then the navy lost interest in Harwich as it was no longer needed as a deep water base for battleships. Even in the early 1950's when I arrived here as a boy on a bicycle I was puzzled why this empty dock was ever built in this forgotten corner. I also visited my uncle who was struggling to make a living from farming Beach Station Farm. From his fields it was possible to look out across the open marshes and see Marriage's Mill outlined against the sky beside the dock. Thirty years later the whole area had become container parks and offices, one of which my own daughter worked in. The 'Dock' at Felixstowe had undergone a total transfor-

Felixstowe Dock started to expand away from the original Dock Basin in the 1960's. Landguard Fort is on the point at the bottom and Dooley Fort was then still to the north of the Dock. (Source: Peter Warren)

mation in just three decades.

In the 1953 floods, Landguard Marshes were flooded and an eye witness account described the scene as the water crashed into the low streets and caravan sites behind Felixstowe, "In the darkness all that could be heard was the roar of the water and the screaming of terrified women." In all, twenty-eight people were drowned in the Beach Station area.

The floods did great damage to Felixstowe Dock's piers and this set back the plans of Mr H. Gordon Parker, a Norfolk corn merchant who had bought it from the government in 1951. Gordon Parker and his general manager, Ian C. Trelawny saw in this silted up dock all the possibilities that Tomline had seen. The policy at the dock changed from steady decay to expansion and attracting more trade. For the first few years their efforts in turning shipping round quickly and cheaply passed largely unnoticed, but suddenly in the 1960's Felixstowe Dock began to attract a lot of trade. This period was a watershed in the development of the British cargo handling industry. On the east coast of England the two large ports of London and Hull had been dominant for over a century. At these ports nineteenth century methods and attitudes still prevailed. In the 1950's London dockers had, by striking, been able to paralyse subsidiary east coast ports. The dockers under militant leaders refused to accept any changes in the ways that cargoes were handled and they fought very hard to prevent the introduction of containers. The more the London dockers slowed cargo handling down, the more shippers looked in desperation for alternative ports. Felixstowe Dock was the first place to really prove this and later most of the east coast ports followed suit.

Perhaps starting from nothing enabled both sides at Felixstowe to overcome the traditional anti-management attitudes of dockers in the established ports. Financially it paid the quay workers at Felixstowe to back their management because they were earning more than their ever striking counterparts elsewhere.

The increased use of road transport also greatly favoured Felixstowe. Lorries from the Midlands could reach the east coast quicker by avoiding going through the miles of traffic jams in the London docks. In the early 1960's the Felixstowe Dock supporters were vigorously campaigning for better road systems to link Felixstowe to the British industrial areas. Even in the days of bulk handling Felixstowe had been attracting goods from South Wales and even Glasgow and Edinburgh, but when the port got tooled up to handle containers it really took off.

The original Tomline dock was enlarged and then in 1965 the new roll-on roll-off service began from a new quay, reclaimed in front of *The Little Ships* and the old seaplane base. Lorries drove straight on to the ferries here which took them to Europort and Antwerp. On the Orwell side of the dock the Admiralty had built oil storage tanks between 1910-13 and they are believed to be the first bulk liquid storage tanks in Britain. In 1956 the new management of Felixstowe Dock started to put up more storage tanks and expand the tanker trade.

In 1968 the Transatlantic Container Terminal was opened and the spin off from the new quays and increased trade was such that the Landguard Marshes had offices and warehouses sprouting up at an

The European Gateway alongside the roll-on roll-off terminal at Felixstowe. This ferry sank just off Felixstowe in 1982 after a collision with another ferry. (Source: Peter Warren)

Felixstowe Dock celebrated 100 years as a working port in 1986 and had one of their former steam cranes unload a token cargo from the sailing barge Beric.

astonishing rate. Felixstowe Dock had about it the atmosphere of a frontier boom town with haulage companies and shipping agents springing up and then collapsing in the fierce competition. The freight at Felixstowe Dock always kept moving, while in the Port of London bitter inter-union wars and union-management wrangles stopped freight and pushed costs up. In 1985 it was possible to drive beside the Thames from Tower Bridge to Barking through miles of empty dockland with not a single ship being discharged, and this had once been the world's largest port. While the Victorian white elephant at Felixstowe had become, by using new technology and with a good work force, Britain's industrial miracle of the mid-twentieth century.

Felixstowe is really two different places, the neat seaside resort and the busy port, both resulting from highly imaginative periods of expansion, yet it remains a level headed down to earth Suffolk town.

CHAPTER FOUR

LORDS OF THE MANOR

Thursday used to be market day in Woodbridge. The Corn Exchange was open every week and the cattle sales were held on alternate Thursdays. Although, within recent years, stall holders have re-established themselves on the Market Hill, Woodbridge had lost all importance as a market centre by 1900. The organisation of large sale yards at Ipswich, and better transport, killed off the Thursday Market.

Woodbridge was the market centre for two distinctly different areas. The modern A12 road roughly marked the border. To the west lay the thickly wooded and heavy clay lands known as High Suffolk. A wheat growing area with huge Tudor farmhouses and little villages nestling in the valleys between well cultivated fields. To the east lay the sandy light lands of the coastal belt called the Sandlings. This was vastly different to High Suffolk; almost flat, it had a few trees, enclosed fields were situated on the better land but for the most part it was open and only grew 'breaks' (a dialect word for bracken). The Sandlings were frequently swept by the bitterly cold east winds (and still are). Under a huge backcloth of open sky, flocks of black faced sheep wandered constantly seeking out every blade of grass. The heath was parcelled off into areas known as Sheep Walks which supported vast flocks and the Sandlings were as remote as the Australian outback.

The 18th century enclosure acts probably did not bring as much hardship to the East Suffolk villagers as they did to those in the rest of England. Although there was a great deal of enclosing, much of the wasteland had already been taken over by individual 'pioneers'. However, when the Earl of Stratford tried to enclose 60 acres of commonland at Snape, one John Woolnough brough a lawsuit against him and won. The real reason why enclosures did not upset the county was that at the end of the Viking era Suffolk had formed part of the 'Danelaw'. Here the manorial system was different. Instead of having one Lord of the Manor, each village was split up into several small manors. These, over the course of time, became small independent farms and the wasteland was gradually added to these. It is very hard to trace any large commons. The strips of land let to manor tenants were often really like large allotments.

In the late 18th century most of the land was divided into farms but agricultural practices gave very low returns for the labour involved. The fashion was to grow three white straw cereal crops and then to leave the land fallow for a year. This was known as making a 'summerland'. On poorer land it was necessary to leave a 'summerland' every other year on this system. The fallow land was ploughed and later cultivated to break up the land and kill the 'rubbish' (weeds). This meant that vast tracts of cultivated land were unproductive and it was not until the famous Norfolk four course system was evolved that this practice was abandoned. Worked out by Coke of Norfolk, this simple system was to grow root crops or beans instead of leaving the land fallow. For East Anglia's largest industry, it was a major breakthrough.

The first golden age of farming was in the Tudor period when the thriving yeoman farmers built fine half timbered houses. Locally this meant that High Suffolk became dotted with attractive houses. The next burst was from the Napoleonic wars until the Repeal of the Corn Laws in 1843. During this time the Sandlings changed from being used for sheep grazing to corn growing, particularly barley which was in demand for making malt. The wealth of that era of agricultural well being is reflected in the local architecture. Most of the Sandlings farmhouses were either re-built or considerably enlarged in the first half of the 19th century. This boost for arable farming created a demand for more workers and many rows of red-bricked cottages were put up.

Looking through the account books of the Ling family at Otley Hall, covering the period from 1745 to 1842, one gets the impression that the pattern of agriculture altered little. Everything was done by hand. I think there have been more technical advances in the last 25 years than in the whole of that 100 years. The book-keeping of these accounts had me beaten to begin with until I realised that the books had been started at both ends and worked towards the middle. These records contain bills, sales, settlements with workers, harvest contracts and parish poor rates.

Corn was thrashed out on the barn floor in the winter with a flail, called 'a stick and a half' in Suffolk. It must have been back breaking work and no doubt if done on 'daywork' too much time was probably spent leaning on the barn door discussing village politics. Therefore, nearly all farm work of that day was done on a piecework basis.

Melton Street in 1905 with the old Wilford Hundred Jail to the right.
(Source: Suffolk Photo Survey)

William Ling of the late 1700's paid his men 6½d a 'cum' for barley, 6d for oats and the princely sum of 1s. 1d. for a 'cum' of wheat. These were the good old days when 'tobacco' was 1s. 1d. a pound and a man cut an acre of barley for 1 shilling.

At the time of the Napoleonic Wars prices seem to have doubled. Boys were employed much more to fill the gap by men away fighting. The boy Hammond worked a seven day week scaring rooks and crows for 3s. 3d. Perhaps we can picture the boy Hammond, a cheerful but ragged urchin, tramping over Otley's heavy fields of spring corn, 'a-shouting' and a-hollering fit to bust'. Few could have got much rest from this method, boys or crows, for as the boy Hammond chased them off Otley Hall, the boy Sam on the next farm chased them back again!

The farmers continued to plough up more and more wasteland, but with the Repeal of the Corn Laws the home market collapsed as soon as cheap foreign corn was shipped in. The population of the whole county continued to rise steadily throughout the 19th century, but in purely agricultural areas the population dropped from the 1840's on. There were 620 people in Alderton, an arable district in the Sandlings, in 1844. Forty years later this number dropped by 100 and by 1921 it had fallen to 426. The same thing is true of many villages, the people just drifted away to look for work. Farming picked up sharply during the 1914-18 war, only to plunge into an even worse slump in 1920.

The worst harvest was in 1879; what a dismal year it must have been for the countryman. Three quarters of the hay and clover was spoiled, since most of it was on low lying marsh land, simply carried away by the floods. At Framlingham passengers had to be taken to and fro to the station by rowing boat.

After months of rain the harvest was begun. A wet harvest is something which has to be experienced to be understood. Days rolled by without anything being done. Corn was flattened by heavy rain, ears began to drop off. At last the weather broke and out everyone went into the fields; but not for long. Black clouds soon built up in the sky and it was not long before the first drops of rain fell. Another day slipped by.

So it was in the year that the British and Indian armies were fighting to gain control of Afghanistan. In the middle of September there were a few fine days and what was left of the corn harvest was gathered in. At 9 o'clock on the 17th September, a thunderstorm broke out, killing a cow on Dunningworth Hall marshes and another belonging to Mr Chaptine at Sudbourne. Richard Rope of Sudbourne Lodge wanted to get his bullocks home from his Leiston marshes, but this was delayed for several days because the roads were flooded in between. Luckily he managed to get them home and yarded before the bad storms of 23 and 24 September.

Perhaps it is not surprising that the older generation were religious men, but there was no love lost between Church and Chapel goers. In the second half of the last century, Mr Leggett tells us in his diaries, which he kept when he farmed with his father at Bucks Hall, Rishangles, and later on his own at Worlingworth, how he and his family went to Church every Sunday. Once during a wet spring drilling he left work at 2 o'clock on a fine day to go and hear a Mr Hammond preach. A month later he again left work to visit the Church, This time to give bread away to the poor. A few days later he drove his daughters into Eye to have their hair cut and give a cheque to a Mr Warner to be invested. Through reading Mr Leggett's diaries, one can see how fond he was of shooting. He and his neighbours had much pleasure this way. This was the true hallmark of East Anglian yeomen. One September they shot all day at Garnham's and only got one bird.

The relief of the seige of Ladysmith in the Boer War is alongside such remarks as 'killed 8 pigs for London'. Pig killing was a monthly event on the farm and I doubt if anybody went hungry in Mr Leggett's household. Of course it was much cheaper to eat food produced on the farm, fancy having to pay 4s. 3d. (22p) for 6lbs of beef as Mr Leggett had to do one day in Framlingham.

Entertainment, apart from shooting, was very limited. The highlight of the year was the Harvest Horkey. Everyone went to Church and sang 'All is safely gathered in'. But the real climax of the farming year was the Horkey Supper. This supper was given by the farmer to his men and was held in the farmhouse or barn. In villages made up of small farms, everyone clubbed together. At the end of September in 1885, Mr Leggett records going to Mr French's for a committee meeting of the Worlingworth Harvest Home Supper. The following Sunday they had two collections for it and raised £4. 4s. 1d. The village craftsmen had their own celebration on Shummacker Monday. On the first Monday after Christmas the shoemakers all got drunk. This seems to have been a very local custom, the origin of which is lost.

During the whole of the 19th century estates tended to get larger and the ownership of land fell into fewer hands. Although some of the older and smaller estate owners lived off the rents of the land, most of the larger ones had money invested in industry and used the returns from this to improve their estates and maintain their high style of living.

A man who went into a London estate agents wanting to buy a farm was asked what sort of farm he wanted – one for hunting, shooting or fishing? With agriculture in a decline, the countryside had become the rich man's playground. In East Anglia the sporting gentry made the pheasant king of the countryside. With the same drive as they used to conquer the world, the Victorians developed shooting – and what startling results they achieved. Prince Fredrick Duleep Singh's 17,000 acre Elvedon Estate recorded taking a 81,877 bag in one season of which 58,140 were rabbits. On one shoot eight guns are reputed to have shot 2,000 winged game in a day. I am inclined to believe that a little bragging went on in the number of game taken on rival estates. However, writers of that time defended shooting. Why, they cried, land that could be let for sheep walks at 2s. 6d. an acre could be let for shooting at a pound an acre. Farming had sunk very low indeed.

In order to achieve the best results the game preservers remodelled their estates. It is no exaggeration to say that the habits of pheasants have dictated the East Anglian landscape. Tree planting became the rage, although FitzGerald complained bitterly that the new-fangled race of squires were cutting down the old woods and banks that bred violets in his childhood.

The cutting down of oaks in the Victorian era was part of the way of country life where everything was produced from the land, but FitzGerald's complaints have a modern ring to them. Tree planting nearer the coast completely destroyed the old open heathland. Miles of Scotch fir were planted to break up the old sheep walks. The Orwell Park Estate planted up much of Nacton and Foxhall, while the Bawdsey Estate employed fishermen and other out of work men to plant up much of the area between Hollesley Bay and the River Deben.

The Bawdsey Estate was created by Sir Cuthbert Quilter. Born within the sound of Bow Bells, he was the grandson of Samuel Sacker Quilter, a large farmer in Trimley. Quilter came to Suffolk for a holiday as a young man. Once when out walking he hitched a lift in a farm cart going towards Felixstowe Ferry. Here he looked out across the Deben at the barren land on the north bank of the entrance and thought that, if he ever made a fortune, that would be the place he would build a house. He did both.

Quilter became the head of Quilter, Barlfour & Co., and member of the stock exchange. At times his financial dealings were on an international scale. In 1873 at the age of 32, he left his home in Surrey where he had commanded the 4th Surrey Rifles and moved to East Suffolk. Here he had the mansion of Bawdsey Manor built. Completed in 1882, this palace by the sea cost him £25,000 and architecturally might be described as a cross between an Elizabethen Manor House and a Maharajah's Palace. It is in a style never likely to be repeated again, but it firmly established Quilter as being a country gentleman. Actually this industrious man could have had little in common with the older and more easy going order of country estate

Bawdsey Manor in 1900 before the trees were planted around it.
(Source: Suffolk Photo Survey)

owners. There is a tradition that for every million he made, Quilter had another tower added to the Manor. There appears to be nine towers.

Since the aristocracy were the ruling classes, Quilter next embarked on a political career and entered Parliament as a member for South Suffolk in 1885. He was popular in his constituency but never reached great heights in government circles. He fought a hard campaign to try and bring in a 'pure beer' act. Although unsuccessful, he tried to prove his point by opening a pure beer brewery at Melton.

Quilter rarely spoke in the House of Commons and presumably he did not rise to a high position in the Liberal Party because of his bitter opposition to Gladstone's Home Rule Policy. He was created a baronet in 1906 (local legend credits him with having three times previously refused a knighthood). This came at the end of his political career as he lost his seat by 136 votes earlier in that year. He had no intention of letting the affairs of the nation pass without his thoughts making an impact. In the years after his retirement, new taxes were introduced which were aimed at the wealthy upper classes. Quilter saw quite correctly that this was the beginning of the end for the landed gentry. The taxes he was forced to pay were only a fraction of what every large privately owned enterprise has to pay today, but he felt that

The Brewery and the Coach & Horses, Melton about 1900 when many public houses still brewed their own beer. (Source: Suffolk Photo Survey)

he was being unjustly treated and announced that the taxes ruined him, he would have to sell his picture collection in order to pay them. His taste for fine art was inherited from his father who had also been a noted collector. The Quilter collection was housed at his London home in 28 South Street, Park Lane and was sold at Christies on July 9th 1909 for £87,780.

This splendid protest against taxation on earnings from individual initiative made not the slightest difference to the course of British political history. The average voter was not in the least distressed to see the proud aristocrats stripped of their finery. Over half a century passed and the whole race of wealthy with unchallenged power were made extinct before the central government began to dip deeply into the wage earners weekly packet. By then the principle of taxation on individual earnings had been long established. I fancy that Quilter, were he still alive, would only comment briskly 'I told you so'.

At its peak his Bawdsey Estate reached 8,000 acres, extending practically along the whole north bank of the Deben. This was controlled by an agent and administered from the estate office at

Bawdsey. Here there were blacksmiths, wheelwrights and building tradesmen. The forestry department had its own nursery and an ambitious planting scheme. The well known stud of Suffolk Punches kept at Bawdsey Hall, carried off prizes at all the local shows, and the flock of Suffolk Sheep won equal fame. The estate was really Quilter's private kingdom but he took his task of looking after the welfare of everyone on the estate very seriously. There was only one sin that could not be forgiven – poaching. If caught, a man could not expect to find another job the Bawdsey side of Wilford Bridge. A tenant farmer who became irritated by having the game eat his crops and ignored the game-keeper's orders to stop netting hares was turned out. Apart from these high handed actions Quilter did a great deal of good. He was the first person in the area to put up good housing for workers.

Once he passed a large group of men standing on Alderton Knoll. What, he demanded from his agent, were men doing standing about in the middle of the day on his estate. The agent explained that they were out of work. Quilter set about finding a scheme to give them employment, pits were opened on light land and the soil was sifted for flints which were used for road making.

One of his shepherd's wives, Mrs Last who lived in the little white weather-boarded cottage on Alderton Walks was very proud of her grandchildren. Quilter offered to give her a shilling for every descendant she could name, a gesture that cost him over two pounds. Much of the estate's day to day running he carried out himself. Once, at the turn of the century, nine corn stacks and the farm buildings at High House Farm went up in glorious blaze. No one knew how the fire started but two points were clear, the tenant's corn stacks were exceptionally well insured but the landlord's farm buildings were not. Quilter pretty soon went round to investigate.

"I just don't know what started it, Sir," said the farmer, standing respectfully with cap in hand. "I just don't rightly know what I'm gonna do come next rent day. All my corn stacks are burnt to the ground...."

Sir Cuthbert Quilter cut him short by demanding if he used a mirror to shave with.

"Why yes, Sir, that I do."

"Then," said Quilter crisply, "tomorrow morning you will meet the man who started that fire."

The Chain Ferry at Felixstowe Ferry.

Once, while on a cruise, Quilter's out-spoken habit ran him into deep water. In Panama, he had an argument with an American. His views of the United States were not complimentary. The American passed on the opinion of a member of the House of Commons to the New York Press and the subsequent rumpus eventually got into the London papers. Anglo-American relationship was a tricky subject, but the Victorians sadly under-estimated the resources and determination of the young America. Perhaps there were some justifications, for Great Britain at that time had controlling influence over at least half the world's surface, while the Americans were still brutally subduing the Red Indians.

Another maritime endeavour was the instigation of the Bawdsey-Felixstowe steam ferry. This may have been prompted by the acquisition of Laurel Farm, Felixstowe on the south bank. Also, when the tide was not suitable to reach Woodbridge, Quilter was then able to cross and use Felixstowe's station. The ferry consisted of two vessels which, because of the very strong tide in the Deben entrance, ran on chains laid across the river bed. In spite of this being well patronized, especially in the summer, 'the bridges' as they were referred to, ran at a loss and finally petered out in the 1920's.

An even more ambitious scheme was to transform the quiet country village of Bawdsey, into Bawdsey-on-Sea, the fashionable resort of the East Coast. This is what had happened to Felixstowe. The little village around the church of Saints Peter and Paul had been pushed into the background as an Edwardian town mushroomed up along the sea front, but history did not repeat itself across the water at Bawdsey.

Quilter collapsed and died suddenly at Bawdsey in November of 1911. He was then 70 years old. His estate had become a well run community, almost a miniature welfare state. The 'good and faithful' estate workers could look forward to protection in their old age and sickness. It differed from the present form of national security in that only the 'good and faithful' received this blessing. The work shy, dishonest and the poacher were not encouraged to stop in the district. Nor was there any nonsense about democracy. Quilter's decision had been final. Everyone was entitled to keep their opinions to themselves.

The social progress of the past half century has made it impossible for any individual (unless he or she has the backing of some powerful organisation) to exercise such strength. This complete change of authority is worth drawing attention to. Today the most difficult art of any individual wanting to put up a house is obtaining 'planning permission'. The would-be private house owner must tread very gently not to offend the local committee or the planning authorities. This system may allow a few horrors to get through the net but prevents a lot more from popping up all over the countryside. However, when Quilter had Bawdsey Manor built, he had the main road re-routed. It was in his way.

The most famous of Quilter's family of seven was the composer Roger Quilter (1877–1953), while the Bawdsey Estate and the bulk of the fortune was inherited by his eldest son Sir W. Cuthbert Quilter (1873–1952). He lived the life of a country gentleman amidst a slowly crumbling estate. In the agricultural depression of the inter-war years the rents of farms could not support the grand scale the estate had been designed to run on. There was by that time a small army of estate workers. The duty of keeping up employment in villages on the estate was still taken seriously, retired retainers were found free housing, no one was turned away. This created a great personal loyalty to the Quilter family, but in the long run it proved financially exhausting, Sir Cuthbert Quilter inherited such a vast wealth and benevolent power

The Harbour Villas at Felixstowe Ferry were among many of the Sandlings houses damaged by enemy action in World War II. However, the radar station at RAF Bawdsey remained virtually undamaged. (Source: Graham Henderson)

Sir Cuthber Quilter (II) opening the new Felixstowe Ferry yacht and dinghy club house in 1932. (Source: Graham Henderson)

that he must have found it almost impossible to realize that the money could ever be spent.

Bawdsey Manor was the first sacrifice. Apart from employing sufficient staff to maintain this small scale palace (to have not maintained it properly was unthinkable), there was also the constant trouble with the encroaching sea. For even after the thousands of pounds the Quilters devoted to shore defences, the short grey waves of the North Sea still tried to gnaw it away from the Sandling peninsula and still today the breakwaters have to receive regular attention if the age old battle is to be won. Bawdsey Manor was finally sold to the Government in 1936 and it was here that a team headed by Sir Robert Watson-Watt developed radar.

The Bawdsey Estate eventually succumbed to the ravages of death duties. The grandson of the 'right old Sir Cuthbert' Quilter, Sir Raymond Quilter (1902–1959) was the last man to head the estate while it was intact in its original form. Sir Raymond was a second son and was brought up to believe that he would have to make his own way in the world, but his elder brother died and he eventually inherited. Sir Raymond had the same dynamic personality as his grandfather and, although in many ways a very sensitive man, he possessed the courage of a lion. As a young man he had his own plane and also used to make parachute jumps over Felixstowe sea front to amuse the summer visitors. The parachute was then in its infancy and although these dare devil escapades did not altogether meet with the approval from Bawdsey Manor, he later began the G.Q. Parachutes & Co. at Woking in Surrey, having rightly anticipated that the parachute would play an important part in the Second World War.

What the Quilter domain may have lost in size, Sir Raymond did not lose in originality. His home was the chauffeur's cottage at Methersgate Hall. His own airfield was on the edge of Sutton Walks and his plane is referred to as being 'the best radio-equipped private plane in Britain'. While 'in residence' at London's Dorchester Hotel he had his own standard, a golden pheasant on a red background, flying alongside the Union Jack.

CHAPTER FIVE

FORGOTTEN INDUSTRIES

At the end of the last century gold was discovered in considerable quantities in north west Canada. This was the famous Klondike Gold Rush which drew men and women from all over the world in a desperate bid for wealth. True, Suffolk has never seen a gold rush, indeed in many ways there was a great lack of gold, but there was once a scramble for the natural wealth found in the Sandlings. This was the now forgotten coprolite digging boom.

Coprolite is the fossilized remains of the huge pre-historic animals which once inhabited the earth's surface. The word coprolite comes from the linking of the Greek words for dung and stone – 'Kopros' and 'Lithos'. Dung stone is literally what it is. The gigantic sharks and dragon like creatures consumed vast amounts of smaller fish and animals. After this food was digested the excreta dropped to the ocean bed and slowly changed into phosphate nodules. The sharks too eventually died and sank to the bottom and their bones became phosphatised. This mixture of excreta and bones built up to a depth of 9 to 12 inches and in one of the world's great earth movements was tossed on to the surface of East Suffolk and Southern Cambridgeshire.

The first recorded use of coprolite as an artificial manure was in 1717 when its phosphatic value was discovered after it had been spread on fields at Levington by Edmund Edwards. No doubt it was used locally from then onwards, but in the 1840's the real coprolite boom began and lasted for the next 50 years. Edward Packard of Snape started the first mill there in 1843 and began to turn coprolite into superphosphate of lime which was sold as a valuable fertiliser. Packard later built a factory at Bramford, by which time other men had joined in the feverish activity and coprolite digging spread rapidly.

The beds of Suffolk crag in which the coprolite was found sometimes lay only a few feet below the surface. Enterprising contractors hired or bought land known to contain coprolite, took on gangs of labourers and sold the 'dung stone' to the mills which were opened up in Ipswich. At first contractors merely dug in the crag that was easily obtainable and then moved on but later on these places were often re-dug. All the work was done by hand and the crag was often removed in wheelbarrows. The most economic workings did not go below 20 feet deep, but in the 1880's contractors were forced to go deeper. The deepest pit in East Suffolk was one of a hundred feet deep dug at Foxhall.

There were attempts at tunnelling but these proved unsuccessful because the Suffolk crag was liable to collapse. Also the use of pit props in the shafts made it too expensive for the amount which could be dug this way. A great deal of crag had to be moved and sifted to obtain an economical quantity of coprolite. The crag was carted out of the pits in horse drawn tumbrils to the washer. Here the nodules were extracted and then despatched to the factories for processing. Another method of extracting coprolite was to flood the workings and then horse harrow the bottom, drain off the slurry and pick up the nodules from the ground by hand. This system however, was unpopular with farmers because land flooded with slurry never recovered. It is said that even now the sites of the old washing plants can still be traced where there are unproductive areas on light land near the old pits.

Landowners naturally did not wish to have their land permanently ruined and in later digs no damage was done to the soil structure. Often it is impossible to trace where the coprolite was removed from, which is probably why the industry is so completely forgotten. The latter day method was to remove the topsoil (all still done by hand) then dig out trenches collecting the coprolite. This process was then repeated about every 20 feet when the topsoil had been replaced. I know of fields done in this way at Bawdsey where it is impossible to see any signs of the former workings. The only knowledge of it was by oral tradition.

Financial wealth was not the only kind unearthed, for countless fine and well preserved fossils of pre-historic creatures came to light. In the coralline crag S.V. Wood discovered 396 species of shells of which 144 are now extinct and many others were Mediterranean varieties which are thought to have lived in a moderately warm sea of 300–400 ft. deep. In many sections of the ordinary Red Crag unfossilised shells are common and in this crag 248 different species have been identified.

To try and date the coprolite workings is difficult. In the Woodbridge area coprolite digging began in 1845, but this appears to

After the cement factory closed at Waldringfield in 1909 recreation boating took over.

have been simply working the crag very near the surface. Digging in earnest in pits must have begun about 12 years later. In the 1870's 10,000 tons a year were being dispatched from the riverside quays of the Deben and Orwell to the Ipswich factories. At Levington, cottage gardens were being dug and lucky owners often obtained a bonanza of £20, probably the value of the cottage at that time. Most East Anglian Museums have a collection of these fossils, Roman remains were also found in coprolite pits. Workers were fond of finding shark's teeth, polishing them up and hanging them on their Sunday watch chains. The pit workers also laid aside intact fossils for sale to collectors.

Almost all the labourers for these pits were local men recruited from the farms. When a labourer on the land was earning 11 shillings a week a pit labourer was getting up to £1 a week. This was on a piece-work basis of 1½d. to 4½d. per cubic yard. True, the coprolite workers had to do more hard shovelling than on the farms, but they never seemed short of willing recruits. At one time £2.10s. was obtained for a ton of coprolite and as much as 300 tons an acre was dug. Land owners no longer sold their land, but leased the digging rights to contractors. The competition was fierce and a land owner often got from £120–£150 per acre for the privilege of having his land worked. At a time when coprolite had sunk to 24s. per ton it was costing 8s. to 10s. per ton although I have been unable to discover what the cost of transport to factories was. Possibly as much again, but this was in the 1890's when the end was in sight. At Waldringfield, where over 1,000 tons were taken from fields behind the *Maybush* all workings closed in 1893.

The industry finally collapsed dramatically at the turn of the century. Phosphates surface-mined in America and shipped to this country proved far cheaper than what could be laboriously extracted from Suffolk crag. Home producers could not compete and many contracting firms went bankrupt overnight. Some workings were left unfinished and the topsoil not even replaced. Machinery was left to rust and men searched elsewhere for work. It did not appear to create a great social upheaval as the scale of the workings had grown smaller.

There was a brief period in the 1914–18 war when some pits were temporarily opened and worked by machines and several thousand tons were dug. But imports started again in 1918 and these operations quickly faded out. In the 1930's some farmers reopened the pits and spread crag on their land as a cheap form of fertilizer. Apparently this was done to try and kill mayweed (the presence of which often indicates sour soil), but the spreading of crag by hand was expensive and of little use. Apart from the numerous pits which are still dotted about the Sandlings little has survived, but in the long run it has done the district good. The surviving Ipswich factories united to form Fison, Packard & Prentice, the chemical fertilizer manufacturers. This in its turn progressed into Fisons Ltd. of which the fertilizer manufacturing section is now part of Norsk Hydro. By one of those odd twists of fate the line of events has done a full circle. For it was at Levington that coprolite was first used for fertilizer and now Fisons plc has its Research Station in the village.

Another industry which is often overlooked is malting. The process of maltings is to make grain suitable for brewing, distilling and a wide range of other uses by forced germination. Since malting barley grows well in the Suffolk climate (in the pre-irrigation days it was one of the few crops which could be grown well on very light land) the industry has always been locally important. But since maltings are often unattractive buildings, plain brick on the outside and gloomy interiors, they have not attracted much attention; although since Snape Maltings has received publicity, interest has been aroused.

Malting seems to have progressed since around 1860. Until then almost all the malting carried out was on a very small scale. As the 19th century grew older the large brick built maltings, many of which are still a feature of the landscape, began to mushroom up all over East Anglia. In the last 20 years, the old hand methods have been replaced by mechanized processes and the industry is now concentrated in fewer, far larger units.

Practically all Suffolk towns had numerous maltings. Woodbridge is reputed to have had 30. Most of them are now untraceable but there is no reason to doubt their existence for many of them must have been 'one man' maltings, simply part of an out-building of a large house or behind an inn; a reminder of the days when every landlord brewed his own beer. There are still several of the steep slate roofed kilns to be seen around the town, but the largest were Waterloo Maltings (now Ingram Smith's builder's yard) and Melton Hill Maltings (now called the Deben Mills).

Another industry which quite naturally was to be found in this great corn growing area was milling. The milling of wheat for flour is not a forgotten industry, but grinding it by wind and water power certainly is. The sight of a windmill's sails turning slowly against the background of a vast blue sky was a common sight to former·generations. When William Cobbett entered Ipswich on one of his *Rural Rides* in 1830 he counted no less than 17 mills at work. He was delighted, and from a man quick to point out faults this was quite a compliment. Enthusiastically he described them, the mills were painted white or whitewashed and the sails were black. This colour scheme seems to have been reversed later because most mills which survived into living memory were black (tar) with white painted sails.

The sight of a windmill at work held a fascination for Edward FitzGerald. There appears to have been three windmills standing on the hill behind Woodbridge in his day. Once when one of these was under threat of being dismantled he purchased a piece of land to prevent this happening. Keene wrote that this definitely made him one of the 'right sort'. But although FitzGerald saved one mill he could not save them all. When large roller mills were established at the ports with an unlimited supply of imported grain coming in, the slow stone grinding village mills were doomed.

Even in 1933 Suffolk had 64 mills working, 29 water and 35 wind. Norfolk had 60 mills relying on wind and water power and most other counties far less. Woodbridge is lucky in having one of the few surviving windmills. This is Buttrum's tower mill which was built in 1816 and repaired in 1954 by the East Suffolk County Council and the Pilgrim Trust at a cost of just under £4,000. There was also a move at one time to restore the tower mill just off Theatre Street, but the owner of the coal business and the ground surrounding it did not want intruders into his yard. Tower Mill stands on what was once Black Barn Farm and the mill was worked until around 1920 by John Tricker.

Like Tricker's tower mill, Burgh mill has also had its cap and sails removed. In this case the operation was carried out in 1934. Previously there was another mill sited slightly to the east of the present Burgh mill which was constructed of red bricks, some of which are now the Mill House garden wall. The last miller at Burgh is reputed to have kept his money under the floor and always wore a top hat when he went to market – as befitted a man of real substance.

One of the unusual facts about windmills is that they were sometimes dismantled and moved to a fresh site. Gedding mill was moved twice the last time was from Felsham in 1867. Bedingfield mill came from Oakley and Tannington mill was first worked at Framlingham. Wingfield postmill was dragged on wooden rollers three miles from Syleham by 20 horses.

While the 1930's Depression stunted all progress, windmills lingered on as part of the country scene. It would have been a great pity if they had all been pulled down as soon as their usefulness was over. Rex Wailes stated that the East Suffolk post mills were the finest of their type, not only in England but in the world, and fortunately one of these has survived at Saxtead Green. The first mention of a windmill here occurs in the Framlingham survey of 1309. Quite when the present mill was built is not known, but the records of one standing on this site go back to 1796. The mill house was built in 1810 by Robert Holmes and the last miller was Mr A. S. Aldred who died in 1947.

During Mr Aldred's time a steam traction engine was used to drive the mill when there was not enough wind. Often during the winter the traction engine was used out on the farm to drive the thrashing drums, 'throsh'en tackles' we used to call these, and after the farm men went home it was returned to the mill to drive it all through the night. It returned back to the farm again the next morning. Mr Aldred also owned a windmill at Worlingworth and during the First World War the fan tail of this was painted patriotically red, white and blue. Saxtead

Green Mill, however, has always been painted white and blue and very attractive it looks. Actually the old millers often referred to their mills as 'she'. Wind driven mills and ships have many things in common; both require skilful handling to prevent them from being overpowered by this fierce element. In 1951 the Saxtead Green Mill was placed in the guardianship of the Ministry of Works, has since been overhauled and is now open to the public.

Suffolk is a county of slow running streams, but this did not prevent them from being harnessed to produce power. Water wheels were put to a much wider usage than windmills, which usually only ground corn or pumped water. The Old Paper Mill at Bramford for instance was worked as a paper mill from 1717 to 1793 and then up to 1880 was also used for corn milling. Glemsford Mill was built in 1825 as a silk-throwing mill. Hoxne Mill was used to produce textiles, flax, linen and grind corn before it closed in 1928.

It is thought that in the middle of the 19th century there were 27,000 watermills in the British Isles. As far as Suffolk is concerned the sites of 73 watermills have been definitely identified. Although this is a large cereal growing area and naturally a centre of the milling industry, once cheap imported grain began to arrive at the large ports towards the end of the nineteenth century, watermills steadily declined in number. Even in 1933 there were 29 water and 35 windmills working the county, which was slightly more than in any of the neighbouring counties. By 1968 the only remaining working mills were Baylham, Layham, Pakenham, Raydon and Wickham Market. There does not seem to have been any pattern of mill closure. Nothing dramatic happened, they just faded away.

The Bucklesham Mill does not appear to have been worked after 1930 and four years after this it was adapted to a pumping station to supply Felixstowe with water. Shottisham Mill, which in 1536 was the home of Bathelmew the miller, was worked up to 1952. It was restored as a private house in 1984.

At the head of the Butley Creek stands a water mill which has been owned by the Hewitt family for several generations. The original Butley Mill is thought to have been sited some two miles further inland near Staverton Park and to have been moved down in 1535. The present mill was driven by an undershot wheel; that is, the water passed under the bottom of the wheel. Rarely in East Anglia were there any overshot wheels with water coming from the top, because of the lack of fall. At one stage a windmill stood on the high ground just behind Butley Mill. After this was pulled down another one was dragged by horses from Martlesham. This mill was destroyed by fire which was a common fate for windmills. The friction on the wooden mechanism being the cause. Following this in about 1890 it was replaced with a roller mill beside the watermill. Further down on the opposite side of the creek once stood a wind driven drainage pump.

In the mid-Victorian period the flour from Butley Mill was taken to London by horse and waggon, but in the 1890's sailing barges, because of their flat bottoms, were coming up the Butley River to load at a jetty about 500 yards below the mill. Lupins, which were one of few crops to survive on the light land at Wantisden, were shipped by the Hewitts to Belgium for dye making. In 1985 Butley Mill was one of the few country mills remaining in business. While other small milling businesses had long since vanished, Hewitts, by patching up second hand machinery managed to keep costs down. They supplied the Hewitt-Sewell farm with pig food and catered for the small, but highly specialized market, in pony and goat foods.

"Do you know about the miller's hair?" asked John Hewitt, the Butley miller. While I was still trying to puzzle this out he went on.

"A good miller was always rubbing the flour in the palm of his hand to see if he was grinding it well enough for his customers, he rubbed the palm so much that a hair started to grow there. Of course this only happened with an honest miller, but then only a really honest man can see the miller's hair."

The country people used to take their corn to the miller to be ground into flour and it was an ancient, if not very popular, custom for the miller to take a 'toll' out of every sack ground. The toll was a set size, but country people always suspected that the miller was taking more than his due. This friction was the source of endless stories, like the one about the miller having a 'golden thumb' because when selling flour he put his thumb into the measure to reduce the volume.

In medieval times the great lords and religious orders got control over the right to use the streams and rivers which drove watermills. This gave them a very powerful hold over the country people because it was very difficult to get corn ground into flour it they were turned away from the mill. The introduction of the windmill in the eighteenth century undermined at least part of the great estate owners control, because anyone with a hill could put up a mill. Indeed in East Anglia

John Hewitt in Butley water mill in 1980. The country mills lost their flour trade when everyone switched to white bread which could only come from modern roller mills. Butley produced wholemeal flour until 1914 and then switched to animal feed.

and other corn growing areas just about every village had a wind or watermill.

The waters of the River Deben drove six mills at one time and the tidal waters at Woodbridge drove another one. Starting up river, the Kettleburgh mill had three 'stones', but there often was not enough water to drive them. In about 1873 a smock mill was moved from Tuddenham so that when the miller was short of water he could use this windmill. However, there must have been periods during the summer months when both mills were stopped. When Kettleburgh Mill was dismantled the wheel was taken to Shottisham Mill and used as an overshot wheel but most of the smock mill parts were taken to Parham Post Mill.

Further down there was a small mill at Letheringham. Mr Cooper installed a small Whitmore & Binyon roller mill plant here, but the vibration shook the building so badly that it had to be abandoned. The roller mill plant was moved to Kelsale where it was installed in a gutted tower mill; but again it was unsuccessful as the machine was too far away from the prime power.

From Letheringham the Deben winds its way down between the low water meadows to the Deben Mill at Wickham Market. The deeds of this building go back to 1701, but it is quite possibly older. Robert Martin, the Beccles millwright who looked after this mill for many years, always maintained that the water wheel was of a type usually made long before the earliest deed date. This wheel weighs 12½ tons and has a diameter of 16ft. When I visited it in 1968 it was still being worked daily and so too was the iron pit wheel which was installed in 1880. This is typical of the slow moving gears of a mill, they seem to have rumbled on for decades, requiring little attention.

The Deben Mill had sufficient water to be worked for 24 hours a day except perhaps during a very dry summer. However, it was once run in conjunction with a four common sailed windmill. This mill was pulled down in 1868 and the bricks were used to build a steam mill. In 1885 the milling business was taken over by Reuben Rackham and he put up the Deben Roller Mill, about 40 yards east of the watermill, to take the record harvest of 1893. The steel roller method of milling wheat was perfected in central Europe in the 1860's and when later introduced into England the traditional stone grinding system was doomed to extinction. It is an odd twist of fate that the Deben Roller Mills ceased to work first in 1949, while the watermill continued in use.

The Deben Roller Mill was driven by a steam engine manufactured by Whitmore & Binyon, which was a local firm which had its head office at 64 Mark Lane, London. Their machines all proudly bore the address of their works at 'Wickham Market, England'. The engine which went into the mill when it was built is 25ft. long and has a 9ft. 6in. flywheel. Since being taken out, its owners have very kindly presented it to the East Anglian Museum of Rural Life at Stowmarket.

The milling business was operated by E.R. & R.T. Rackham Ltd. whose activities were not wholly confined to grinding corn. The watermill was still worked because of the interest taken in it by Reuben Rackham's two sons Edward and Robert Rackham. Edward Rackham began work at the Deben Mill in 1910 and he was the only man left who knew how to work it. The flour ground there was sold to

The Rackham's Deben water mill at Wickham Market in 1967.

local bakeries. Although the mill had three stones, each stone weighing 8 cwt., only two stones were worked at once. Edward Rackham was told that the three stones used to be worked all at once, but this had never been done during his time. He believed that it would throw too much strain on the great crown wheel. This massive wheel has 120 wooden cogs which were renewed in 1927. Mr Rackham lived in the house on the end of the mill and did not get iron cogs because they would have made too much noise.

A little further downstream is another mill which the Rackham's were connected with. This was rented by Reuben Rackham and later the Rackham brothers worked it for three days a week and the owners, Loudham Estate, worked it for the other three. Edward Rackham always knew it as Ash Mill, he worked this until 1956 when it was preserved. It never had any other power except water, an unusual feature was that it could be driven with only 2ft. of water at the sluice gates. In the summer the Rackham's only had enough water to work Deben Mill during the day and in the evening one of them cycled down to Loudham and used the same water to run that mill.

The name Ash Mill was probably used by the millers because it was simple to say, but it was also referred to as Campsea Ash Mill, was Ash Abbey Mill and quite recently Loudham Mill. The original mill was

In 1900 the sea and the railways were the main links with the outside world. The schooner English Rose lies in the Ferry Dock and passengers hurry away after leaving the steam train at Woodbridge Station.

built by the Augustan Canons of Campsea Ash Abbey, which was founded before 1195. The remains of this priory are near Abbey Farm House and here in 1843 six stone coffins were dug up. The remaining two mills which stood on the Deben have both been turned into attractive houses. Both were quite small mills, the one at Ufford ceased to work in 1916 and the last miller from Melton Mill moved to Ipswich in about 1896.

The Tide Mill at Woodbridge is one of the most unique industrial buildings in Britain. It has had a long career spanning nine centuries of usefulness. it must have provided flour for many generations of people living in the town. The first mention of the Tide Mill was in 1170 when the canons of Woodbridge Priory granted Baldwin de Ufford a plot of land so that he could have easy access to the mill. These early records do not state the type of mill, but since no possible alternative site has been found for de Ufford's mill, it is assumed that it stood in its present position. This is the first known record of a tide mill in the British Isles.

Before reclamation, the Deben must have reached further inland. Station Road must have originally been a track just above the high tide mark. Presumably a medieval quay reached from the Boat Inn to the Tide Mill. At that time a small stream which started in the grounds of Woodbridge School flowed down across the Thoroughfare down Brook Street and ran out into the Deben on the southern side of the Tide Mill. In 18th century prints the course of this stream can still be seen coming out near the mill. The stream is now piped but originally it must have washed away silt and kept the berths open.

For a long time it was thought that the Tide Mill dated from the same period as the 'Bell & Steelyard' in New Street. However, the Steelyard, which was used for weighing corn, was erected in 1674 while more research suggests that the present Tide Mill was built in about 1793.

The workings of Woodbridge mill do not differ from an ordinary watermill. The difference lies purely in that the tidal water was trapped in the pond on the in-coming tide and used to drive the mill during the following ebb tide. Some tide mills had ponds which were also fed by fresh water, but at Woodbridge the mill relied solely on its seven and a half acre pond of salt water. The work done in the Tide Mill was of course tidal and once the flood tide had covered the ferry hard there was not sufficient fall of water to turn the wheel. The mill had four stones, although there is said to have been enough power to drive all four at once, only three ever worked together during the last years that the mill functioned.

In a map of 'Town and Port of Woodbridge' drawn by Suffolk Surveyor, Isaac Johnson (1754-1835) in 1827 the mill and its granary appear to be just as they have survived until recent years. No doubt at first only local grown corn was ground at the mill, but by the end of the 19th century imported wheat was being brought here. When A. Hayward & Son traded as corn merchants from here they expanded the business by building a steam mill where there was a reliable supply of water, opposite the gas works. There was then regular barge traffic bringing up wheat, although the flour was not taken away by water after the 19th century. Arthur Thorpe, who as a young man worked as a docker, known as a 'humper' at Woodbridge, recalls that barges were unloaded by a gang of six men. The operation was carried out by hand, two men down in the barge's hold, two men on the winch lifting the sacks to deck level and two men carrying sacks on their backs up a plank to the second storey of the granary. They reckoned to unload a barge in a day and a half. It is doubtful if any wheat was brought in by water after 1926.

In about 1932 the Tide Mill wheel began to give trouble. The existing wheel had been put in by Collins of Melton some 80 years previously. A new wheel was built on the old shaft by Amos Clark. This millwright was closely connected with the mill during the last years it was in operation. Amos Clark was born in 1875 at Weybread and his family owned land at Debenham. He learnt the trade of a millwright from his father, the secrets of this craft having been handed down successively from his great-grandfather. As a young man he worked in London, but during the First World War he brought his family back to Suffolk. He established himself at Woodbridge and looked after Tricker's, Buttrum's and the Tide Mill. (Mills seldom had names but were known by the men who worked them). Just at the end of the war he moved to Charsfield and then to Parham. Here he had the blacksmith's shop and also owned the Mendlesham Post Mill, which was worked by his brother George. Next Amos Clark moved to Grundisburgh and while he was there he pulled down Mr Nunn's mill.

After the war there was a great shortage of seasoned oak, which was in demand for putting the face on mock Tudor Houses. Amos then employed up to eight men and during the following two decades he pulled down over 80 wind and watermills in the Eastern Counties. This must have been a sad task for men whose real vocation was to repair them. Fortunately not everyone wanted their mill destroyed, it was a job that could only be done once. Amos did rebuild four mills which included Thorpeness Mill.

Apart from the Tide Mill wheel, another of his accomplishments was the construction of a huge pit wheel for the Duke of Grafton's Sapson watermill in Buckinghamshire. This was in about 1942 by which time Amos had settled at Belle Vue Road, Ipswich. He built the Sapson wheel in his tiny back garden. The neighbours were most intrigued as Amos's handmade masterpiece took shape. At the time his family were not impressed, as the operation ruined the garden and it caused quite an upheaval when the wheel had to be taken apart in sections and carried through to the road to be loaded on to the lorry.

In 1950 he repaired the famous Pakenham Mill near Bury St Edmunds. This is a fine tower mill and had been damaged in a gale two years previously. Amos restored it to working order with full sails and went on working as a millwright up to the end of his 78 years. All his four sons were apprenticed to his craft, but later went into other

Nacton Decoy man George Skelton and his trained dog with duck from the trap end, 1904.
(Source: R. More)

worked in Britain dropped from 200 in the early nineteenth century to 46 in 1886 and to 28 in 1918.

The opening of Abberton Reservoir in the 1930's drew away so many wildfowl from the Blackwater that the remaining decoys were no longer worth working. The Grange decoy at Tillingham was the last decoy working in Dengie Hundred it was probably still being worked after World War II, but this has now been filled in like so many decoys. The last one to be worked commercially in Britain appears to be the Nacton decoy on the north shore of the River Orwell. This Suffolk decoy was worked right up to the 1966 season.

While most decoys are on flat marsh near an estuary, Nacton is in a valley and started as a mill pond which was developed into a decoy in 1835 to catch duck for sale. The number of pipes were made up to four by 1860 and in about 1880 a smaller Teal pond was dug. At this time it was on the estate of Colonel George Tomline who had encouraged the building of a railway line to Felixstowe so that the town could be developed as a seaside resort. It seemed that the owner of Purdis Hall decoy claimed that the railway had ruined his income. As the railway line ran only 350 yards away from his Nacton decoy Colonel Tomline made a point of continuing to take large numbers of duck and took 17,991 fowl in eighteen years, a record year being 3,000 fowl. He brought in one of the Skeltons, the great decoy builders. George Skelton had come from Lincolnshire in 1807 to make the first improved Dutch-type of decoy in East Anglia, at Winterton. His great grandson George Skelton worked Nacton decoy until 1919 and then it was worked by Tom Baker until 1966.

The Nacton decoy was then leased by the Wildfowl Trust who used it for ringing duck, mainly pintail and widgeon, right up to 1982. They gave it up then because the creation of the new reservoirs, particularly Alton, had drawn the fowl away. From the 1950's the Wildfowl Trust had been ringing duck at Borough Fen decoy but the creation of the massive Rutland Water reservoir took away the waterfowl.

By 1984 the Nacton decoy was still usable. Iken decoy was used as a Battle School area during World War II and was then bought by James Mann of Bawdsey and he returned it to a morning flight pond for duck shooting for sport. He also had part of Sudbourne Great Wood cleared for food production. In this wood the bulldozers unearthed a man trap capable of breaking a leg, recalling the days when village life was dominated by a running battle of wits between the 'game preservers' and the poachers.

CHAPTER SIX

TRADE INTO THE RIVER

Woodbridge and indeed the whole Sandlings seem to have prospered
in the sixteenth century when the enterprising tudor merchants
grew wealthy on Europe's gread demand for wool. The first Custom
House was erected on Woodbridge Quay in 1589, but in the next
century it was moved to Quay Street. By then the port was thriving
with annual revenue from Suffolk cloth at £2,722, a considerable sum
for that period.

With Woodbridge shipping expanding, the port began to come into
its own as a shipbuilding centre. The main reason for this was the
forests of prime oaks growing on the heavy land of High Suffolk. Ships
were doubtless built here in Tudor times, but the 17th century saw an
enormous demand for timber, especially in the Thames shipbuilding
yards. But transporting such ungainly logs proved a major problem. it
was easier to build the ships at Woodbridge than cart the timber to the
Thames. The first people to bring this piece of logic to a conclusion
were the Pett family. Trading ships of note were being built before they
took an interest in Woodbridge but, once the Petts gave their support,
things expanded rapidly. The Petts were extremely numerous,
possibly originating in Harwich, but by the 17th century they were
well established as shipbuilders on the Thames, mainly in the king's
service. In 1599 Phineas Pett became master shipwright of Deptford
where he built the *Prince Royal,55* guns, in 1610 and between 1635–37
the famous *Sovereign of the Seas.* These were then the finest ships afloat
anywhere in the world and no doubt there was a great deal of Suffolk
timber in both of them.

While on timber buying expeditions in Suffolk, Phineas Pett often
lodged at Thomas Cole's Crown Inn, Woodbridge. He eventually
arranged for his fifth son Peter Pett (1610–1672) to marry Cole's
daughter. The marriage took place in 1633 and through his wife Peter
Pett gained property in Woodbridge.

Between 1625 and 1638, 11 ships of substantial size were built in

The lighthouse on Orfordness is one of the wildest and least accessible places in East Anglia.

Woodbridge, the largest of which were the *Levant Merchant* and *Muscovy Merchant*, both of 400 burden tons. The *Prosperous Mary* built about 1635 was taken to Deptford to be rigged and later came back to load 171 tons of provisions at Woodbridge Town Quay for the army in Scotland. Peter Pett became Master Shipwright at Chatham and later as Navy Commissioner was allowed to give contracts for the building of men-of-war. He saw to it that some of these went to Woodbridge: Thomas Adams, Edmund Munday and William Carey all got much sort after contracts.

The first ships built for the navy were the 4th rater *Advice,* 544 tons, 230 men, 48 guns, and *Reserve,* 513 tons built at Woodbridge in 1650 at a cost of £6. 10s. per ton. The practice was that after the vessels were launched (the *Reserve* drew 15ft of water) they were towed or sailed under jury rig to the Thames for fitting out. The builder appears to have been under contract to supply the ship partly manned. Local men however, were not keen on the navy and preferred to serve in the

Ipswich colliers where, even if the pay was bad, at least they received it.

Adams had trouble finding enough workmen to finish the frigate Maidstone and when she was completed he had to take command of her, The Dutch were then doing all they could to stop the coastal shipping and often large fleets of merchantmen lay in Harwich harbour. The *Maidstone* was employed guarding the coast after a Dutch frigate had chased a hoy into Woodbridge Haven. A hoy was a passenger carrying vessel and the Woodbridge Haven is still marked on some maps at the Deben entrance.

Even if the Dutch wars caused a great demand for naval vessels, Woodbridge as a coastal town bore much of the burden in Britain's struggle for maritime supremacy over the Dutch. Munday travelled to Woolwich to try to obtain the money owed for some timber he had sent. In 1653 General Blake landed 300 sick men with orders for them to be cared for by the people of Woodbridge. The arrival of these meant higher taxes for local people to support them. Many of Munday's and Carey's shipwrights promptly fled from the district. The town already had Dutch prisoners on its hands and it had also incurred heavy losses in a law suit against the Seckford family over the almshouses and trust money, all of which amounted to the town being in debt by £500.

While Oliver Cromwell remained Lord Protector, much attention was paid to the strength and general efficiency of the navy. In 1654 the 4th rater *Preston* 516 tons was launched at Woodbridge, just a year after the *Maidstone.* On the restoration of the monarchy in 1660 many ships were renamed; *Maidstone* became *Mary Rose* and was finally captured by the French in 1691. The *Preston* became the *Antelope* and was sold in 1693. The Woodbridge ships served the navy well, although at times their masters appeared to have used them as privateers rather than for any high minded ideals of being instruments of national security. Only Edward Russell, who at one time was master of *Reserve,* rose to high rank. This colourful admiral destroyed the French fleet at La Hogue for which he was created the Earl of Orford.

On the announcement in 1660 that Charles II was to be made king, the bells were rung in St Mary's, Woodbridge. One man, however, still spoke well of the protectorate and was promptly taken before the magistrates and was ordered to keep good behaviour. At the time of the restoration steps were taken to make the measurements of ships

The site of Woodbridge Riverside Theatre was a warehouse and stables in 1905. A boomie barge waits for a high tide to get into the Ferry Dock.

more accurate. Since Elizabethan times general confusion had grown up around the method of classifying ships by their tonnage. In theory the term 'tons burden' described the amount a vessel could carry. The reformed system of 1660 still only gave a rough estimate which made vessels on their tonnage measurements seem smaller. Therefore, Woodbridge built ships such as the *Darling* of London 350 tons, *Resolution* of Aldeburgh 300 tons, and *Protection* of Ipswich 200 tons were in fact a good deal smaller than their tonnage suggests. Another case is the *Goodman,* built in 1634, which is described as being 700 tons, but she would not have been nearly the same size as a modern coaster of that description.

There was no lack of work for the town's shipwrights. From 1630 to the end of the century 15 men-of-war were launched here, and repair work was also done. While *Centurion* was being repaired in 1658 her bowsprit broke and six men were drowned. In 1666, when the plague swept through the town killing over 300 people, the frigate *Albermarle* was launched. It must have been a difficult time to complete a wooden ship. The labour requirements were enormous; every piece of wood had to be sawn by hand.

Although Woodbridge was near a plentiful supply of oak the lack of water must have made launching a large ship difficult. Certainly Harwich and Ipswich began to take the lead. Also Peter Pett ran into deep political troubles. Following the custom of the day he gave the lucrative state offices to his near relations. His enemies would no doubt have done the same, but in the end they had him thrown out of office. However, the town's reputation must have been quite good, for the building of warships did not quite end with Pett's dismissal. In 1675 the largest vessel ever built on the Deben was launched into the little tidal estuary. This was Edmund Munday's 4th rater *Kingfisher* 663 tons. Later she took part in the capture of Gibraltar and ended her career as a hulk at Harwich. The last warships from the town's yards were the 5th raters *Hastings* and *Ludlow* both 381 tons and 32 guns, built at the closing years of the century.

There is a description of the town in *Suffolk Traveller* written about 30 years later:

'Here are two quays, the common quay and where the chief Imports and Exports are, and where the fine 'Woodbridge' salt is made, and above this is the Lime-Kiln Quay where formerly the Ludlow Man of War was built. Some years hence another Dock below the Common Quay, where the Kingfisher Man of War was built, but this is now (cut) from the River by a mud Wall and almost filled up.'

The 18th century is something of a blank as far as Woodbridge maritime history is concerned. The town remained a port and shipbuilding centre, but few records of that time have survived. The only shipyard was the Lime-Kiln yard and this then covered the strip of ground running from the Deben right up to the Thoroughfare. Timber was stored at the top end and the ships were constructed where the Lime-Kiln Road houses now stand. The actual Lime-Kiln stood on the ground between Gladwell Dock and Sun Wharf. This area's connection with the timber trade lasted until the 1920's for little Scandinavian square riggers used to bring cargoes to Messrs. Brown's yard which then occupied what is now the down river end of Robertson's yard. Like all the deep draught vessels which visited Woodbridge, the Norwegian brigantines had to discharge part of their cargoes into lighters at Kyson Point.

Shipbuilding has always been a precarious occupation. In 1751

Edward Darley went bankrupt, although his property included the Boat Inn and Anchor Inn he was apparently building at the Lime-Kiln yard. Samuel Turner took over and built ships as well as being a timber merchant. In 1764 he built a 240 burden ton ship for the Jamaica trade. This was the largest built in the town after the men-of-war, but the capital outlay must have been too much for Turner. Perhaps the buyers did not honour their agreement. Bad debts can ruin any organisation. But whatever happened, Turner went bankrupt not long after the ship had left the Deben.

The next builder of note to operate at Lime-Kiln was William Dryden in 1796 who built ships for the coasting trade and a few larger ones such as the packet *Henry Freeling* for the Harwich-Hook of Holland passenger and mail service. For the first half of the nineteenth century a steady stream of tubby little brigs and schooners were built at Woodbridge. They seem to have been employed in the coal trade to the north of England or in the days before railways they went to Liverpool after oil cake for cattle food. Some went to the Baltic after timber. The last trading schooner built at Woodbridge was the *Ellen* in 1853 and the last one afloat and trading was the *Bernard Barton* which was lost in the Bristol Channel in 1899.

The population of Woodbridge in 1801 was just over 3,000. The town prospered and by 1851 the numbers had risen to over 5,000, then suddenly they began to drop. There was no future and the people began to move away; however, the coming of the railways stabilized the situation and the population remained much the same until the 1930's. When various light industries grew up in Woodbridge the population began to increase again. Thus in 1959 when the *Woodbridge Reporter* celebrated its centenary, the town's population was almost the same as when this newspaper was established.

There had been an earlier newspaper, the *Woodbridge Advertiser* started in 1843, but this had only appeared every four weeks. The *Reporter* was very much more up to date as it was a weekly; it must have been born on a wave of optimism for it began the same year as the railway reached Woodbridge. The history of the railways is really part of the national development, it ended the town's importance as a self-contained unit.

In 1794 one coach a day and a weekly wagon passed through the town on the way to London. the coach took 13 hours to reach its destination but this situation had very much improved by 1844 for by

Woodbridge as a busy port in about 1910.

then 12 coaches, omnibuses, carriers' wagons and carts passed through the town each day on the way to London. To travel from Woodbridge to London then took five hours and it cost 10s.

The railways did not meet with everyone's favour. There was a slight commotion when the East Suffolk Railway bought the Lime-Kiln area in 1856. A man named Smith was running a boat yard where the Cinema now stands at that time. This was all swept away and so too were the ancient salt pans where salt had been extracted by evaporation. Possibly the reason for having the station just near the quays was really because it was easier to get the track level on the flat ground next to the Deben. When the railway started in 1859 many people believed that this was the end of the town's usefulness as a port. But in fact shipping went on for another 60 years and it was the road transport that dealt the knockout blow.

Water-borne transport was usually cheaper than the railways, but it was also very unreliable as it solely depended on the weather. A ship could take two days or two weeks to reach London, or in the winter two months, but for bulk goods like coal and corn, time was not so important and in 1883, 346 sailing ships and three steamers brought 22,968 tons to Woodbridge so it was still thriving as a port. Two years later there were 219 commercial vessels registered there giving employment to 350 men and boys. This is a slightly misleading number because many were Aldeburgh and Orford fishing boats. Fishing boats registered at Woodbridge had the letters 'WE', but in the 1880's the Customs & Excise closed the Woodbridge Custom House and fishing boats were registered at Ipswich with the letters 'IH'. At least one Woodbridge smack proudly carried her 'WE' letters into this century.

When trading schooners of Woodbridge and Orford were sold, lost or became worn out, the shareholders did not turn to sailing barges, they gave up. The trouble with the Deben and the Ore was getting over the bars across the entrances. A sailing vessel had to pick the tides carefully to get in and out of the smaller Suffolk estuaries, but they could sail without delay right up to Ipswich in any weather. There were six pilots living at Felixstowe Ferry who, between a bit of fishing and going out salvaging in bad weather, made a living by getting barges over the murderous Deben bar. The pilots kept their 15ft boats on the beach in front of the Martello Tower. They had many tricks for getting a barge in and even when the weather was too bad to get out the pilots anchored on the inside of the bar channel and signalled with flags which way the barges should steer.

Barges frequently lost time laying off at anchor for days waiting for the right conditions and some were damaged and even lost crossing the bar. The ketch barge *Lord Hartington* was swept ashore by the tide at Felixstowe Ferry and the pilots had difficulty hauling her off. The spritsail barge *Emma Mizzen* was going into the Ore estuary in front of Shingle Street when a sudden wind change caused her to sail at full speed into the shingle. The impact was like striking a rock and the bows burst open and she was lost. The schooner *Rudolf* was owned by the Nortons of Shingle Street when she ran aground and was wrecked in front of the houses. She had been trading to the north for coal and 'over the other side' to Holland and France. The Shingle Street man Beeton was always glad to get a berth in her to earn a little money. However, the wooden hull was worn out and the crew had to pump almost continuously and in port they emptied sawdust bags round the hull which was sucked into the seams and stopped the leaking until she

The 184ft motor cruiser Scarcity dragged her anchor during a snow storm in 1960 and went ashore at Bawdsey. She was later towed off.

'worked' in the next blow. In 1953 the sea washed away the shingle at Shingle Street and revealed the gaunt remains of *Rudolf.* I saw her clipper bow there in breaking water at low tide, a haunting memorial to the long gone era of small sailing ships.

The sailing barges were so successful on the east coast because their flat bottoms allowed them to get into shallow rivers and creeks sooner than the deep draught schooners and steamers. Also the spritsail rig, with its numerous winches allowed just two men to control a very large sail area. There was a whole fleet of sailing barges trading between the Waldringfield Cement Works and the Thames, and the Essex barges came in to collect hay, straw and mangolds from farm wharves or 'docks', as they were always called in the Sandlings, which were taken to the Thames to feed the London street horses.

A barge could, with her flat bottom, sit on the mud anywhere. At Iken Cliff the barges sat on the beach and the crew and local men used wheel-barrows to take the cargoes ashore down planks. At Shingle Street and Bawdsey, shingle was loaded straight off the beach.

Boyton Dock, Ramsholt Dock and Methersgate Quay were large enough for one barge to lay on the end while Hemley Dock, which was cut in the saltings by a local farmer Charles Cooper in about 1896, took two 'stackie' barges. The tiny Bantam Dock at Martlesham, now virtually silted up, and Stonner Quay, now almost washed away by the channel which broke through the saltings during World War II, are other Victorian barge quays.

A man who 'ran away to sea' in the days when every tide carried a barge up to Woodbridge was Arther Hunt. He was the son of Sir Cuthbert Quilter's head gamekeeper and, unknown to his parents, signed on in a boomie which was discharging coal at Ramsholt Dock. After this he went on up to Woodbridge in the barge to help them finish unload. Arthur's parents walked six miles to plead with him to come home. In the end, after all the arguments over the follies of a sailor's life had failed, they bought him sufficient clothing to help him on his way. Later, he went into Parker's barges, first as a mate and then briefly as skipper on the *Dover Castle,* and also went as one of the racing crew on the *Violet Sybil.* Following a disagreement with Clem Parker he left and joined the Fowey schooner *Alert* at Ipswich and voyaged to Newfoundland. During the First World War he went into steam ships, but after a lung injury, returned to his home estuary, the Deben.

Arthur acquired a philosophy of a man trained in sailing ships and developed a considerable talent at spinning a yarn. He was the last professional yacht skipper on the Deben in Captain Gilbey's *Genesta.* In the winter, the *Genesta* was laid up against the broken down barge quay and Arthur made nets in the cabin for Aldeburgh fishermen and weekend trawlermen. I spent many hours during my school holidays sitting in the cabin listening to yarns about the 'old days'. He was glad of someone to talk to as he worked away at his trawls in the snug little cabin. His face was weatherbeaten to a walnut colour but the top of his forehead where his cap went was always white.

One thing Arthur did give me was his father's recipe for poisoning rats. Now the parish always seems to have suffered from an excessive number of rats and I had long heard of old keeper Hunt's ability to kill them with a secret mixture of which he would never divulge the contents. What I was solemnly presented with was a very faded piece of paper on which a Norwich chemist had written a reliable rat killing bait, back in the 1880's. It had been treasured by the Hunt family until, as there were no longer any gamekeepers in the family, it was

Sailing barge Dawn coming into the Woodbridge Tide Mill berth in 1986. Frank Knights is in his boat helping.

passed on to me. I was very flattered but never dare put Hunt's poison into action. It started off harmlessly with 'one peck of fine barley meal, sifted,' but the real knock-out ingredient is capable of killing every living creature for miles around.

How I wish that I had written down some of the stories that Arthur Hunt told me. Perhaps the best tale was that of the fate of one of Mr. Bloss' bullocks. Around about 1912 the *Pacific,* one of Goldsmith's of Grays barges was laying in Melton Dock when its skipper and mate discovered that they had developed that recurring human phenomenon – they had spent all their money. Perhaps this was a common occurrence for this pair – perhaps they could not get a 'sub' from the owners. In this unhappy state, they sat on the barge's forehatch with nothing else to look at but a bunch of Mr. Bloss' fat cattle grazing on the marshes.

Now the mate of this barge had at one time been a butcher's assistant and he must have been the prime mover of that night's dishonest work. They drove a bullock up on to the Dock, roped it up and killed it in the old pole axe manner; in the darkness they bled the animal into the ebb tide and then by lamplight they cut the carcass up in the hold. Next they went up to Wilford Bridge and woke up the crews of three of Parker's barges, which were laying there with cargoes of stone, and sold them meat. The same was done in the Ferry Dock and by dawn every barge in the upper reaches of the Deben had parts of the missing animal hidden aloft in their tops'ls.

Strange to say this crime was never detected, although the police must have had a shrewd idea of what became of the bullock. The following midday they entered the 'Boat Inn' and began questioning all barge men and riverside workers who were there playing quoits; one constable was even reputed to have remarked that he could smell an extremely good joint in the oven. Never did such an obvious clue get overlooked.

Sometime early in this century Captain Robert Skinner began to play a part in the maritime affairs of Woodbridge. He had been master of the large schooner barges *Zebrina* and *Belmont* which were owned by the Whitstable Shipping Co. Then Skinner started on his own as part owner of the boomie *Lord Alcester* with the coal merchant Cox. The Deben was a good place to establish a barge owning enterprise. After all, there was no one else attempting it. Skinner's method of retailing coal was to sell it straight out of the barge in small amounts. It was easier for the village people to buy it at riverside quays than to collect it from Woodbridge or Melton stations. Word went round when Skinner was in the river and anyone wanting coal took a horse and tumbrel or even just a wheelbarrow down to the waterside to buy some.

Captain Skinner's three sons went into his barges. John skippered the *Lord Hartington* until he took a job in North Woolwich, Wesley was mate with his father in the *Lord Alcester* and later owned the *Martin Luther* and *Nautilus*. George, the youngest of this sea going family, first 'went away' in the *Zebrina* when she was rigged as a barquentine. Later he came back to Woodbridge to help with the family coal business, but could not settle and went off again, into steamers. He became a quarter master in the P & O lines and then changed to the continental ferry service from Harwich before he came back to barges. He even took the *Dover Castle* which was not a coasting barge, up to the Humber after coal but preferred taking *Lord Alcester* with coal from the Tyne to the Biscay ports. This barge carried five hands and an average passage took nine or ten days. After this he went as skipper in Cranfield's Ipswich grain barges, having the *Venture* for quite a while, but he did not like spritty barges; they were never out of the sight of land for long enough.

The last work Captain Robert Skinner could find for his barges was to carry shingle up from the Deben bar for building material. This really was flogging a dead horse, since every vessel had to earn its own replacement value and shingle carrying barely gave a living wage. It did not even keep the *Tuesday* in good order; she drifted up and down on the tide with sails in pieces. It must have been a sad blow for the old Captain. He had played an important part in the development of the sailing barge and had commanded some of the very finest craft back in the 1890's. But he did not give up, in fact he died, aged 82, aboard the *Tuesday* off Green Point in 1935.

George Skinner is still remembered in his retirement role as the Woodbridge ferryman. Before the advent of the car and bus country people travelled by foot and there were many ferries over the Deben and Ore/Alde, most of which have vanished and the rivers have become barriers. There was a ferry over the Deben from Woodbridge to Sutton in Tudor times and for centuries people walking to Woodbridge market from the Sandlings villages went this way rather than the long route over Wilford Bridge. In Issac Johnson's map of Woodbridge in 1818 the ferry is shown as running at low tide from a hard in front of the Tide Mill to one still just traceable opposite, on the Sutton shore. While at high tide it ran to the end of the Ferry Quay. In the 1845 Admiralty chart there is another hard marked beside Mill Creek but in 1874 another hard and a river wall leading to it was made on the Sutton shore.

In the late Victorian era the ferry was a vital link in preserving Woodbridge residents all important respectability because a guide book tells us 'The bathing place for men is on the Sutton side', referring to the sandy beach which then existed below Sutton Ferry Cliff. While the male population swam and exposed a limited area of naked flesh over the river, 'The ladies are provided for at the Lime-Kiln Quay Swimming Baths' which had been made by simply walling up one of the docks there. The good people of Woodbridge did not, in the

The Woodbridge Ferry leaving the Sutton hard in about 1908. (Source: Rick Hogben)

halcyon days before the Great War shattered the old order of class and respectability, indulge in anything as risky as mixed bathing. The ferry fare across seems to have been 'three pence', but in bad weather, when two men were needed to row the boat, the fare doubled. At low tide the river was virtually empty so a flat (punt) was used, but the ferryman still had an awful job pushing the flat across. The demand for the ferry was such that right up to World War II the ferryman paid for the privilege to operate it.

Sir George Manners, who built Little Haddon Hall in 1914, gave the right of the ferry to the Woodbridge Urban District Council in 1925. When Frank Knights ran the ferry after World War II it had become a service supported by Woodbridge Urban District Council grants. The council tried to close it and held a Town Poll to see if anyone wanted it. Everyone who used the ferry voted yes, but the rest did not vote at all. When the council next tried to close it, Mr. Pelly brought and won a High Court Action in London to force them to continue to run the ferry. By this time George Skinner was being paid to run the ferry and keeping the takings but he refused to divulge to the council just how many people used it. Finally George died and Frank

Knights took it on again, but in 1974 the new Suffolk Coastal District Council stopped paying for a ferry.

This ferry stopped because no one had a reason to cross the Deben, but in 1984 new excavations started at the Sutton Hoo ship burial site and it was suggested that the ferry should be re-opened to make a more interesting way to visit the site. A great many people wanted to see the ferry re-opened so that when the Sutton Hoo Society asked me to attempt to re-establish it, my main task was to co-ordinate that goodwill. Now it runs on summer weekends when the tide is high and for parties that have been booked at suitable times.

CHAPTER SEVEN

THE HERITAGE OF THE COAST

In June of 1783 the *Templar* and the *Flora* raced from Woodbridge to Bawdsey Ferry and back for a 'valuable silver' cup. After this there was a lunch at the 'Queen's Head'. The event got some publicity because some unsporting character stole one of the contesting craft. There was quite a fuss about this but it looks as if the craft was eventually returned. Whether this race was between yachts or passenger carriers is not certain. However, it does appear to be the first mention of racing on the Woodbridge River. Racing of one sort or another has been going on more or less continuously ever since.

The Deben Yacht Club was founded in 1838 and by then there was a small nucleus of yachts kept on moorings off the Ferry Dock. Some of these were the *Rival, Syren* and the *Pearl.* About the same time the *Helen* made a cruise to Holland from Woodbridge. The shipbuilders must have been responsible for many of the yachts, William Taylor built the *Osprey* and others, no doubt. Garrard built a six oared galley for 'gentlemen to row'. Rowing was a popular pastime until after the First World War and featured quite prominently in the Woodbridge Regatta. In 1854 there was a £3 purse for the winner of skiffs of 18 feet, while the four oared boats shared a purse of 10 sovereigns, seven for the first and three for the second, which suggests that the numbers entered were not very large.

The method of handicapping yachts in the same regatta was to give half a minute for every ton over 12 tons. In the small class the same system was used for every ton above 6 tons. The yachts competed for a purse of 10 sovereigns, plus 5s. added by the Deben Yacht Club. All very simple, but I have no doubt there were arguments! In the evening there was a dinner at the Crown Hotel, then a fete and fireworks display on the Crown Bowling Green. In 1872 the annual river event was enlarged and called the Grand Woodbridge Regatta, and afterwards there were still the usual festivities in the town. The Deben Yacht Club then appeared to be administering the Regatta and were also holding sailing and rowing matches frequently.

The peaceful uncrowded River Deben at Woodbridge in the 1930's with the Iron Duke discharging shingle at Ferry Dock.

Many people go afloat to escape organised society and one of the Victorians to enjoy cruising was Edward FitzGerald who lived in Woodbridge and was a 'gentleman of considerable private means' able to devote much of his time to sailing. His best known yacht was the 14 ton schooner *Scandal,* named he said after the chief product of Woodbridge. *Scandal* was built at Wivenhoe in 1863 and there seems to have been little or no yacht building at that time in Woodbridge. It appears that shipbuilding had stopped at the Lime Kiln Yard and one end had become a timber yard. Schooners from the Baltic used to come up and anchor off Kyson Point and timber was brought up by lighter. The other end of this waterfront was taken over by Ebenezer Robertson in 1884 and the founding of the Woodbridge yacht building industry stemmed from Robertson's which over the decades trained many of the shipwrights. There was still a boat builder working in Brook Street and he built the skiff *Teddy* in about 1875 for the pilot Marsh to row down and meet the ships coming up. The *Teddy* is the oldest Woodbridge built boat still in existence.

At the Lime Kiln Yard the channel cuts in close to the bank making it the best place to launch ships. Also on the flood tide one can get afloat before it is possible to at the Tide Mill or Ferry Dock. Ebenezer's son, A.V. 'Robbie' Robertson gradually expanded yacht building and the yard became well known for the barge yachts it built, the largest being the *Esnia* in 1909. They also built the launch *Monare* in 1904 which was probably the first motorboat built on the Deben. The yard was run after World War II by Bertie Robertson, Robbie's son.

Ebenezer had hoped that his son-in-law Alfred Everson would go into the Woodbridge boatyard, but he quarrelled with Robbie Robertson so instead Ebenezer, who had a coal merchants business at the Jetty started Everson boat building here in 1889. This jetty was used to discharge barges with coal and timber to save the difficulty of getting further up river. Another attempt to save the port of Woodbridge was by cutting Loder's Cut in 1879 to cut out the difficult Troublesome Reach below Kyson. This was originally narrow and shallow, but has been getting steadily deeper and wider as the tide sweeps through.

In 1912, when Alfred Everson was fifty years old his yard was burnt down destroying two yachts, eighteen open boats two motor boats and everything in store. The old sheds had been on top of the river wall but they were rebuilt as the Phoenix Works, after the mythical bird which rose from the fire. When Everson's sons Cyril and Bertie started work at the yard in 1914 they received two shillings (ten pence) a week and had to work from sunrise to sunset. Alfred was also piloting barges up to Wilford Bridge with stone for road making, but the barges were already giving problems going through the yacht moorings.

The Eversons were well known for building 12ft gunter clinker dinghies and the 3 ton Cherub, a cabin yacht for estuary cruising. Between 1923-36 some twenty-two Cherubs were built and these were the first generation of the class yachts. In 1969 the yard changed hands and Peter Darby became Managing Director. His enthusiasm for steam has lead to rallies for steamers being held here and he has restored his own clipper bowed steam yacht *Myra*.

By far the best known yard in East Suffolk for many years was Whisstock's Boatyard. Claud Whisstock went to sea in steamers just after World War I but could not get a berth during the depression. He did a spell with Robertson, worked at Brook Marine, Lowestoft until

Launching of the Glee from Everson's Boatyard, Woodbridge in 1960.

Launching of the aluminium hulled Adaro from Whisstocks, Woodbridge in 1984

the General Strike of 1926 threw him out of work, then returned to Woodbridge and started doing yacht repairs and running motorboat trips to Felixstowe Ferry at weekends. Then he bought a piece of marsh ground between the Ferry Quay and the Tide Mill Quay and built his first workshop on stilts. The area was filled in with frontage to the river, although the yard had a lot of problems launching boats from here.

The first sizeable craft to be built at Whisstock's was the 35ft motor cruiser *Bendor* in 1932. In 1937 the yard started its own class boat, the Deben 4 tonner to a Maxwell Blake design. The war years saw over 200 craft of various types built for the war effort and after this there were a great many repairs to wooden yachts which had been laid up for five years. In the 1950's, Whisstock's were building 'one off' yachts to a high standard. With the introduction of GRP hulls other Woodbridge yards abandoned building new wooden hulls and switched towards repairs. Whisstock's were able to go on attracting orders from all over Britain and North America for new wooden hulls. This became increasingly difficult to do economically, but Whisstock's remained firmly committed to producing new craft. In the 1970's fitting out aluminium hulls was the main way that new yachts were completed. In 1984 the yard seems to have been expanding with a new shed and four aluminium hulls, made in Lincolnshire, were brought down by road and completed in Woodbridge. Unfortunately the Whisstock Boatyard was forced to close later that year, although George Whisstock re-opened the yard the following year and started building new craft.

The wooden boat building tradition was kept alive by a former Whisstock foreman Russell Upson who moved to Slaughden and between 1973–85 built six Aldeburgh beach boats. The one built in 1985 for William Free was 22ft 8in long, larger than normal so that he could fish up to eight miles off Aldeburgh beach.

Whisstock's yard at Woodbridge became the base for David Cowper for his record breaking single handed round the world voyages. In 1979–80 he clipped two days off the 226 day voyage for a west to east circumnavigation, by Sir Francis Chichester. In 1981–82 Cowper again, in his 41ft aluminium *Ocean Bound* made another record breaking single handed circumnavigation. Determined to make another lone voyage, he bought the 41ft ex-Aldeburgh stand-by lifeboat *Mabel E. Holland* and starting in 1984 he became the first man to complete a single handed circumnavigation entirely under power.

Claud Whisstock was always on very good terms with the neighbouring boatyard, Frank Knights (Shipwrights) Ltd., but the two yards could not have been more different in the way they operated. Whisstock's was a 'new build' yard run on industrial lines, while Knights is a group of independent craftsmen doing repair work. Frank Knights grew up in Melton and has early memories of the river. He can remember going down after school and seeing the dredger *Holman Sutcliffe* at Lime Kiln Quay waiting to be broken up. This was an unsuccessful venture and in 1931 her remains were dumped across the river where they can still be seen. In between breaking her up, the men involved used to go down to the Deben entrance in the motor barge *Justice* and load shingle. Ted Marsh, the river pilot, also brought up shingle, 9 tons at a time, in the *Iron Duke* which was then discharged by hand at the Ferry Quay.

Frank Knights worked for the boatbuilders Sharp & Pembethy, just down stream of Robertson's until they closed when World War II started and Frank went fishing in his Brightlingsea smack *Yet* which he had bought in 1938. Actually Frank says that George Green did the fishing and he made the tea! Following this he worked at Robertson's until 1941 when he was released to join the Royal Navy as a shipwright. He then spent three years in the Mediterranean with minesweepers and clearing the channel to Antwerp. In 1948 Frank and Philip Gooch set up as jobbing shipwrights in the end of the Eastern Counties Farmers warehouses at Ferry Quay. The yard has since built about twenty boats, but the main effort has been rebuilding and servicing boats.

In the period between the wars the Deben was an incredibly peaceful backwater. In the 1920's barges and a few steamers were coming up and even Dutch coasters brought dried peas to the Woodbridge Canning Company's Sun Wharf right up to 1939, but the river was mainly left to a few yachts and rowing boats. When there was an attempt to form a committee to control moorings at Woodbridge in 1949, this created great anger and there was a feeling that the Deben should remain totally unrestricted. Each part of the Deben was the 'territory' of some local waterman who controlled it with a rod of iron, but all the time pressure for mooring space was mounting. In 1961 there was a lively meeting at Ramsholt, when the Woodbridge 'total freedom' party tried to prevent a mooring committee being formed there, but eventually a committee did lease

After the 1953 East Coast Floods, caused by an abnormally high tide, the sea defences had to be repaired. Here the river wall is being repaired on the Dock Marshes, Ramsholt.

the river bed from the Crown Commissioners and Waldringfield and Felixstowe Ferry followed suit. In 1985 Woodbridge again looked towards solving its problems, by which time most of the river from Sun Wharf to Methersgate Quay was full of moorings.

While some form of restraint is accepted as a necessary evil to overcome the problems caused by large numbers of boats, the right to navigate freely has been maintained but the Suffolk Coastal District Council and Anglian Water Authority have made attempts to take over control of the tidal Deben. The Suffolk Coastal District Council wanted, in the 1970's, to get rid of the houseboats at Melton and this sparked off the question of who owned the mud oozes between the low water mark and the saltings. Riverside properties on the Deben seem to have undisputed claims to the saltings, but the ooze at Woodbridge and up river had also been claimed by landowners. At Melton the title deeds appear to include the ooze back to the 1790's while in the Lime Kiln Reach the ooze is shown as being part of the town Common in 1594 which stretched up to the backs of the Thoroughfare properties. In the seventeenth century shipbuilding boom, the Common and Lime Kiln oozes were leased to John Mundy for 999 years and it appears that some of the oozes were reclaimed to improve the site for launching larger ships. Woodbridge people had a very long memory because two centuries later when the Ipswich bankers Alexanders, (who seem to have financed most of the shipping at Woodbridge) sold part of the Common to the East Suffolk Railway Company, there were angry public meetings at Woodbridge when they tried unsuccessfully to get the money paid to the town.

Up to the 1970's most Woodbridge and Melton wharf owners and boatyards claimed the adjoining oozes and reclaimed or used them at will. However, the Crown Commissioners, who owned most of the British foreshore, refused to accept some of the deeds at Woodbridge and claimed most of the upper Deben ooze except the Woodbridge Ferry hards.

The upper tidal Deben is a quiet place which holds many secrets in its shallow twisting channel. The Saxon Wufflings chose wisely when they made Rendlesham, above the tide range, the centre of their kingdom. The Deben's habit of drying out at low tide made it very difficult for unfriendly chiefs to make a surprise attack while the Wuffling's own men, with good local knowledge, would have had no trouble getting a boat up here, probably to a recognized royal landing place, above Wilford Bridge, on the hill top near Woodbridge Golf Club, the Saxons had the Wilford Hundred Moot, a place where people met to deal out justice and settle disputes. Even when the Wilford Court moved to Melton, and then Woodbridge, the Hundred Gallows for public hangings stood above Wilford Hollows. A grim place with a long history of rough justice.

After the Saxon times the ships became a little deeper draught and Woodbridge was found to be a more convenient landing place. It was not until the Victorian era, when flat bottomed spritsail barges evolved, that it became possible to get trading craft up to the upper reaches. The Melton Hill Maltings built a barge dock and there was also one at Melton Dock (which was filled in in 1984) and barges with road making material by-passed Flea Island in the bight near Melton Station and sailed or were poled up to Wilford Bridge Wharf.

In the 1960's East Suffolk was shaken out of its isolation by a rapid rise in wealth and better roads, bringing more people into the area. At this time Glass Reinforced Plastic hulls were being mass produced and all these factors combined to produce a sudden explosion in the number of boats using the tidal waters. The digging of Woodbridge

There were very hard winters in the Sandlings in 1929, 1940, 1947, 1955, 1963, 1985 and 1986. Here, in 1963, the River Deben is frozen over right down to Waldringfield, which is the only time it is remembered to have happened.

Yacht Harbour in 1962 and then the opening of the Suffolk Yacht Harbour on the River Orwell in 1970 on marsh which had been flooded in 1942, helped a little to relieve the massive public pressure on mooring space.

The introduction of mass produced speedboats caused considerable friction when in the hot summer of 1976 there were several very dangerous incidents with waterskiers in crowded anchorages. Worried that the hazards afloat seemed to be man made I got up a petition to try and nudge the local authorities into finding a solution. Finally the situation was solved democratically by fixing an 8 knot speed limit on the river except for the Black Stakes Reach near Felixstowe Ferry. When the police on the launch *Ian Jacob* tactfully enforced this limit in 1979 calm returned to the river and the wildlife on the upper reaches stood a fighting chance.

Along the Suffolk coast, wildlife has survived better in this largely agricultural environment rather then in places where industry has increased the population. The return of the avocets to nest on Havergate Island after a long absence from Britain and the establishment of a Bird Reserve there in 1947 is well known. The avocets largely depend on the shallow waters in the Butley River for their feeding ground, while the nightjar can only survive if their habitat in the remaining Sandlings heath survives. The heaths have been slowly eaten away over the centuries.

The Napoleonic War appears to have seen the plough replacing sheep, but then in the late nineteenth century when Australian wool and mutton caused a surplus, the Suffolk Sheep Walks were abandoned and the great estates planted up some areas for pheasant cover and the rest was left for rabbits. World War II saw Martlesham Heath aerodrome expanded and Sutton Heath and Bentwaters USAF bases were established. Martlesham Heath has now largely vanished as it was steadily built over with houses from the mid 1970's.

Other heaths have shrunk, most of Sutton Heath was ploughed up by Sir Raymond Quilter in about 1958 and the Bartons were reclaiming the heath near Sutton Hoo from about 1950–1970. All were under pressure from the Government to get land into production as people could still remember being very short of food in World War II. However, in about 1973 fifty acres of Hollesley Heath was made an official nature reserve for the nightjars.

The old style gamekeeper shot every bird of prey because he was sacked (often on the spot if his employer had a poor days shooting!) unless large numbers of pheasants and partridges went 'over the guns'. Gamekeepers have largely given up this approach and this probably explains the sudden increase in the number of marsh harriers in the early 1980's. Some live quite happily in marsh areas which are intensively farmed but are free of the interruptions from most people.

Since farming is the most important industry in the Sandlings, the way the land is worked has a profound effect on village society. When horses were kings, nearly everyone was in some way connected with the land. The iron makers Page & Girling at Melton actually made farm implements and there were wheelwrights at Shottisham and Bawdsey. Even at the time of World War II there were harness makers at Melton and Alderton and blacksmith's shops at Bucklesham and Bawdsey, to name a few, all dependent on the farm work. Almost all the horses were chestnut Suffolks, nicknamed the Suffolk Punch because of their thick necks evolved for pulling ploughs. This world famous breed was largely created on the Sandlings farms in the early nineteenth century. Every horse in the breed is descended from a stallion foaled in 1768 and owned by a Mr. Crisp of Ufford.

On the heavy land a farm horseman was expected to plough an acre a day with a pair of horses. On the light land a man could do two acres if he did not stop if it rained. The use of the early tractors started to reduce the number of horses and this freed the grassland for the introduction of much larger dairy herds and vegetable crops also increased along the Suffolk coast. In 1980 over production of milk saw most of the herds vanish from the Sandlings and this caused a further drop in the labour forces needed on the farms. In 1953 a 35hp tractor was considered large for farms in this area but by 1985 tractors of 180hp and over were in use ploughing about twenty acres a day. Machines were actually forced on agriculture because the returns for crops sold did not keep up with rising wages and overheads. As the farms repeatedly cut their labour force this had a dramatic effect on the village society. In the fifteen villages between the Deben and Ore (the newcomers have started calling this area The Peninsular, but it is almost an island) at least 300 regular farm jobs and countless part time work vanished due to mechanisation and the abandoning of livestock in the three decades after 1955.

Irrigation completely altered agriculture in coastal Suffolk. It was introduced into the Sandlings after the 1953 floods to try and wash the salt out of the marshes, but it was quickly realised that this was an answer to the country between the rivers which had considerable drought problems. In rainfall terms the Sandlings could be classified as semi-arid and in long dry summers it sometimes looks like a desert, although it seldom gets very warm. To compensate for being virtually the driest part of Britain there is a lack of frost in the salt atmosphere which means that crops can be two weeks earlier than those in the Fens. The use of irrigation and then plastic sheets after 1979 made the Sandlings farmers the forerunners in growing early potatoes and carrots.

The Sandlings villages have adapted over the centuries to many changes in agricultural practices. This is visible in the architecture. Most of the farmhouses were originally half timbered long houses, usually from the Elizabethan period of expansion, which have been added on to. There seems to have been a great burst of building

Unless otherwise attributed all photographs, including the front cover,
are by the author

Some other books from East Anglian Magazine

East Anglian Coast & Waterways
Robert Simper £5.95

A fascinating look at the history of the coast and the inland waterways of East Anglia and how people have used them.

Colchester Through the Ages
J. J. Maling £5.95

This is the story of England's oldest recorded town, written to entertain as well as to inform, and told with wry affection. Serious students in search of cold facts will certainly find them here, but the book is mainly intended for the general reader.

Ipswich Through the Ages
L. Redstone £3.50

Essentially a book for readers who wish to know more about the town than the guide books tell them.

Sudbury Through the Ages
Barry L. Wall £5.95

Barry Wall's first book in this series introducing us to the buildings and streets of Gainsborough's birthplace. Over 80 photographs and drawings.

Long Melford Through the Ages
Barry L. Wall £9.95

This is a book full of surprises. Much has been written about Long Melford before but never quite like this. The author has carried out a long overdue re-assessment of the major buildings, including Kentwell Hall and Melford Hall, and the results are startling to say the least. Over 75 photographs in colour and black & white.

East Anglian Golden Book
compiled by Michael Watkins   £9.95
Extracts from 50 years of the East Anglian Magazine.

East Anglian Journey
Michael Watkins   £5.95
This is the story of an East Anglian Journey. It is also a treasure hunt, the author's footprints leaving a trail of clues which the reader can follow from chapter to chapter.

This Other Breed
Michael Watkins   £3.50
In this book East Anglians talk about themselves – 'mutter' might be a better word, 'We talk with our mouths shut because we don't want to let the east wind in.'

Tour Through the Eastern Counties
Daniel Defoe   £7.50
Daniel Defoe is remembered today chiefly for two works: *Robinson Crusoe* and *Moll Flanders.* He was also a great traveller and an astute observer. What he saw in his travels through Norfolk, Suffolk, Cambridgeshire and Essex nearly 250 years ago is told in this book.

Rum Owd Boys
James Wentworth Day   £3.95
A collection of stories from the Essex marshmen, wildfowlers, poachers, smugglers and fen-tigers, some moving, most wickedly funny.

A Garland of Hops
James Wentworth Day   £2.95
This book is both a sequel to the author's *Rum Owd Boys* and a guided tour of some of the most characterful pubs in Essex and the Suffolk borders.